CYCLING TEXAS

CYCLING TEXAS

• • •

Foreword By
Peter Nye

Taylor Publishing Company
Dallas, Texas

Book design and maps by Deborah Jackson-Jones

Copyright © 1993 by Taylor Publishing

Published by Taylor Publishing Company
            1550 West Mockingbird Lane
            Dallas, Texas 75235

Library of Congress Cataloging-in-Publication Data

Cycling Texas / foreword by Peter Nye.
        p.   cm.
      Includes index.
      ISBN 0-87833-816-0
      1. Bicycle touring—Texas—Guidebooks.   2. Texas—
      Guidebooks.
      GV1045.5.T4C93   1993
      796.6′4′09764—dc20   92-37827
                                              CIP

Printed in the United States of America
10 9 8 7 6 5 4 3 2 1

Acknowledgments

I wish to thank Bob and Andy for their tolerance and all my cycling companions for sharing my curious addiction to this sport.

Ann K. Baird

I want to acknowledge the help and encouragement I've received from the Lubbock Bicycle Club.

Rebecca Kinserlow

I want to thank all the nurses at Big Bend Regional Medical Center in Alpine for saving my life; Beth Garcia at Big Bend River Tours in Lajitas for my housing; Gay Kempf at Desert Sports in Lajitas for a job that allowed me to become intimately familiar with the Big Bend area; Charlotte Allen at the Apache Trading Post in Alpine for information and topographic maps; Jim and Rhonda Hoyt at Richardson Bike Mart for their generosity; and Michael "the two-wheeled" Carr for putting me in touch with this project initially.

George Sevra

Thanks to all of the Road Buddies past, present, and future, who have made the roads of Texas come alive and, as always, to Suzie.

Ed Swan

I would like to thank my grandmother, Elizabeth Greenlee Kelley, whom I called "Mommush," for living in the Texas Hill Country. As I grew up, we took many Hill Country drives together. On the way to fishing spots, swimming holes, peach stands, low water crossings, scenic vistas, *and* visits with her many *Old Stock* acquaintances, she shared her tomboyish lore and spirited love for this unique region with me.

I would also like to thank Lorena Jones, our editor at Taylor, for her generous patience and gentle steerage.

Lawrence Walker

CONTENTS

FOREWORD

Peter Nye

The bicycle is the noblest invention of mankind.

—William Saroyan

I took my first bicycle ride at age five when I accepted a friend's offer to get on his balloon-tired Schwinn, which he pushed to get me going. I was so excited that it never occurred to me to ask how to steer or stop. That ride was such a thrill. I screamed in delight. The white clapboard garage I headed for grew larger and larger. I rode right into it and crashed. In less than five seconds, I discovered two important elements about bicycle riding—it's exciting and there's more to it than just getting on and rolling away.

As with playing tennis or golf, there are cycling techniques that help you enjoy your activity more. Learning them is not difficult the way calculus is. Sometimes it helps just to have someone point them out, like when my friend demonstrated how to pedal backward to engage the coaster brake on his Schwinn after I rode it into the garage.

Bicycle riding certainly has a great deal going for it. Ernest Hemingway, for example, observed that riding a bicycle was better than driving a car to get the feel of the country. He could have been describing the rolling hills of East Texas, but he happened to be on his way to Paris, France, working as a war correspondent for *Collier's* magazine in 1944. Papa wrote, "It is by riding a bicycle that you learn the contours of a country best, since you have to sweat up the hills and coast down them. Thus you remember them as they actually are, while in a motorcar only a high hill impresses you, and you have no such accurate remembrance of country that you have driven through as you gain by riding a bicycle." Hemingway is just one of many writers and artists—from Samuel Beckett to Robert Benchley, Sir Arthur Conan Doyle to F. Scott Fitzgerald, Dorothy Sayers to Kurt Vonnegut, Jr., and Frederic Remington to Marcel Duchamp—who have extolled the bicycle in their work.

Whether you're an adult who has never participated in sports or has considerable training in other sports, and whether you are young, middle-aged, or older, there are a number of practical considerations that will enhance your cycling accomplishments. One is to recognize that the overwhelming majority of bicycles are made for men, although women make up 53 percent of the country's population and need different components in a bicycle.

In buying anything, whether a pair of blue jeans or a bicycle, it helps to know what you want before you enter the shop. Sales staff in the 7,000 bicycle shops nationwide want you to buy the bicycle that is best for you, so it helps to give some thought to what your needs are.

When choosing a bike women should look for a wider seat, narrower handlebars, smaller brake levers, and a shorter handlebar extension to accommodate their body structure. (For both men and women, handlebars should be as wide as the cyclist's shoulders.) These components are easy to interchange and should be done before you leave the store with your new bicycle.

Choices have become more complicated in recent years with a greater variety of materials and bicycle models cascading onto the market. But if you want to ride in the Hotter 'n Hell Hundred in Wichita Falls, Texas, or in one of its kindred recreational rides on paved thoroughfares, then a road bicycle is best suited for your needs. Road bicycles come with frames made of steel, aluminum, and carbon fiber. Steel frames, made of Columbus tubing or other similar materials, tend to weigh more than aluminum or carbon fiber, yet handle better down hills when moving in excess of 45 miles per hour. But aluminum and carbon fiber frames are easier to pedal up hills. Tires on road bikes are an inch or so in diameter, are lighter, and more responsive than mountain bike tires. Road frames also are more lively than off-road frames and more efficient in transferring pedaling energy to forward motion, allowing you to go faster longer.

Most recently a compromise between the mountain bike and the road bike has entered the market. It is called the hybrid because its design is a cross between the rugged mountain bike and the light, responsive road bike. Hybrids are different and hold a certain cachet. Best for short rides of 5 to 30 miles, hybrids combine the lighter frame of a road bike with the straight handlebars and wider tires of a mountain bike.

The relationship between mountain bikes and road bikes in the commercial market is competitive but not fixed, with cyclists choosing one instead of the other. Studies show that people who were introduced to cycling with mountain bikes go on to buy road bikes for longer and faster rides. And long-time road riders take up mountain bikes to go out and explore the flora and fauna where they live. In any case, decide what kind of bicycle you want—mountain bike, road bike, or hybrid—*before* you walk into a bike shop.

□

When the fitness boom began in the early 1970s, more people than ever took up swimming, running, and cycling. Most of the bicycle sales were to adults, who adopted cycling as a recreational sport. What used to be the domain of Olympic hopefuls or children too young to have driver's licenses became more democratic. Adults by the millions took up bicycle riding, incorporating it into their lives the way they turned to art or music to enhance the quality of their life. They became part of the masses on wheels who braved the torrid heat in the Hotter 'n Hell Hundred, conquered the hills in the Muenster Metric Century in Muenster, and tamed the Beauty and the Beast in Tyler.

Part of cycling's charm is that it can be enjoyed alone, with a partner, or as a family. Cyclists have the choice of riding hard or taking it easy. Regardless of how they choose to ride, thousands of them have discovered the fun of participating in recreational rides like the Possum Pedal in Graham, the Border Surf and Citrus 100 at South Padre Island, and the Firecracker 100 in Stephenville.

Napoleon said that even a bad battle plan beats no plan at all, and the same principle applies to preparing for any recreational ride. Start by putting on a helmet. They're lightweight and are good insurance in case you take a fall or encounter a distracted motorist. Preparing for an extended ride takes some time, depending on your physical fitness level, how long your goal ride is, and how much time you have to get ready.

As Martin Meletio of Dallas says, "The fun about cycling is that you get in good shape fairly quickly." He started riding in 1989 and was soon participating in recreational century rides (100 miles) on weekends. A work colleague, Chuck Edds, rode with Meletio forty-five miles one weekend, sixty the next, then seventy-five miles, ninety, and finally the full century. "It seemed like no time before we could ride one-hundred miles straight, without getting off our bikes," Edds recalls.

Their approach as recreational riders resembles that of Tour de France champion Greg LeMond—a consistent training program that doesn't overload the body. When increasing mileage, go up in increments of 10 to 15 percent a week. After four weeks, cut back to your original week of mileage and resume the program again. Training is a form of stress, and it is necessary for the body to recover. Signs of over-training are chronic fatigue, indifference to things that used to matter, and the loss of a sense of humor.

Training with a partner, as Meletio and Edds did, is often a good way to enjoy the outdoors, exchange observations, and talk. Talking has added importance. If you are pedaling too fast or working too hard, you can't pass the talk test—because you're out of breath. That's an indicator to slow down the pace and let the good times roll.

Techniques

Pedaling cadence. Pedal at a rate of about seventy to ninety revolutions per minute. This rate helps your momentum carry you up a hill or churn into the wind. If pedaling faster than ninety revolutions per minute, shift up to the next gear and if slower than seventy revolutions per minute, shift down to the next gear.

Try to pedal in a round stroke. Novice cyclists have a tendency to push hard on the downstroke at the expense of the upstroke. As a result, there is a tendency to bounce in the saddle at the top and bottom of each pedal stroke. One way to determine if you are a "bouncer" is to put some loose change or a set of keys in the rear pocket of your jersey and pedal fast. If you hear the jingle, you are bouncing and should concentrate on achieving a more round pedal action.

One way to help round out a pedal stroke is to leave your bicycle in a low gear and keep your pedals rolling—up hills, over flat terrain, and down hills. Don't coast. Concentrate on pedaling round circles.

Gripping the handlebars. Easiest to overlook in cycling is the grip, but it is crucial. Do your hands get tired? They may be wrapped too tightly around your handlebars. Keep your wrists straight to ease the flow of blood from your arms to your hands. To keep from unconsciously assuming a death grip, wriggle your fingers occasionally and imagine you are holding eggs.

Bend your elbows. Bent arms are a natural shock absorber when you hit an irregularity in the road. Straight arms and a tight grip on the handlebars set you up for a fall, which is easily prevented if you just bend your elbows.

Climbing uphill. Here's a chance to change your riding position for a moment. Most of your ride is made sitting in the saddle. Going up a hill presents an opportunity to use different parts of your leg muscles and to rest the ones that have been doing the work. Generally it is best to limit your riding out of the saddle to about a minute because it takes more energy to pedal upright when your legs are bearing more weight. Racers with heart monitors watch their pulse rate jump twenty or so beats a minute when they rise out of the saddle to pedal uphill.

When you lift yourself off the saddle, move your hands to the handlebar hoods (brake levers). Position your body as you pedal so that your chin is aligned vertically with your knee and foot on the downstroke. This helps you to best use your weight as you work against gravity.

Descending. Put your hands in the bend of your handlebars. This ensures that you are looking up and have immediate access to your brakes. Depending on the length and the grade of the descent, you might also want to try a couple of variations.

For more speed on a road that offers good sight lines and no intersecting streets, put your pedals at three o'clock and nine o'clock so that your cranks (where your pedals fasten) are parallel with the ground. Move your hands to the top of the handlebars near the stem (which holds the handlebars), and flatten your back aerodynamically so that your chin is close to your hands. This cuts your wind resistance and helps you pick up speed all the way down.

To slow your descent, such as on wet pavement, sit more upright with your hands on the brake hoods and your fingers near the levers. This exposes your chest, a major source of drag resistance.

Turning on dry pavement. Take an approach (what cyclists call a line) on the outside lane going into the turn, cut the corner close, and then swing to the outer lane. Put your inside leg up, with your knee pointing in the direction of the turn, position your outside leg down, and lift your chin so you can look forward and take in a good view of what's coming up.

When approaching a turn at speed, it helps to press the foot of the outside leg down on the pedal to give the center of the bicycle more stability. I practiced this a lot while riding down the Rocky Mountains for the first time when I attended the Connie Carpenter-Davis Phinney training camp in Beaver Creek, Colorado. We routinely had descents of 40 to 50 miles per hour on roads that serpentined to take us down 4,000 feet of elevation in thin air that had less resistance than I was accustomed to at sea level. I felt comfortable speeding through turns, at one with the road.

Handling loose gravel or wet pavement. It helps to move your rear end over the back wheel to place more weight on the back of the bike. Set your pedals at three o'clock and nine o'clock so you can sit up slightly and move your rear end back, holding the saddle with the inside of your thighs. Mountain bike riders often shift their center of gravity like this to ride over steep terrain.

Riding mountain bikes is great practice for bike handling in tricky landscape. This is the best way for a cyclist to learn to handle a bicycle when the back end breaks loose and the tire skids.

During a fast descent down Vail Pass in Colorado, at 10,000 feet altitude, I was traveling faster than 40 miles per hour when I encountered a stretch of dirt that a recent rain had washed over my path. Suddenly my bicycle was breaking out from underneath me and I was fighting to keep it upright. At the moment panic flashed through me, but then I was out of the dirt and hurtling along dry pavement again. One of the teenage riders in our training camp whipped by and blurted, "If you were a mountain biker, you would have handled that better." Next time I'll be better in the dirt.

Basic Information About Going on Rides

What to eat and drink for a ride is obviously important, and much of it depends on individual preferences, but there are some things that men and women of all ages and ability have in common. A considerable amount of energy, which burns calories, is used to keep the body at 98.6 degrees Fahrenheit. This means you need fuel to heat your body when it's cold and to cool it when it's hot.

Because Texas can be torrid, it is crucial to keep properly hydrated. Try to curb consumption of caffeine and alcoholic beverages—they tend to hasten urination and reduce your body's fluid level. My breakfasts usually include a cup or two of coffee but I limit myself, indulging in a flavor that I like.

How do you know when you've had enough to drink before a ride? A general indicator is when your urine is clear. (Conversely, a sign of dehydration is dark urine.) On all rides, drink early and often. When you start out drink about six ounces of fluids, which will be sweated out instead of going through your digestive tract. Then continue drinking. Don't wait to feel thirsty.

Riders competing in the race around the Hotter 'n Hell Hundred course will each consume close to twenty sixteen-ounce bottles of liquid to stay hydrated. Keep that in mind when you ride.

Several sports beverages are available on the market. I like Gatorade, but I have to dilute it, two or three parts of water for every part of Gatorade. This is a lesson I learned the hard way. The sugar concentration in it is so high that it gives me stomach cramps on hot days. Some of the sports beverages that are high in fructose also give some people wicked diarrhea, which quickly leads to dehydration. Find out what works for you by experimenting on short training rides.

What you should eat comes down to the basics: balanced meals. Satchel Page, the legendary baseball player from the days of the

Negro baseball leagues, was noted for his counseling against eating fried foods. "They angry up the stomach," he said.

Stick to carbohydrates, such as pasta, rice, bread, and vegetables. Fish and chicken are more easily digested than red meat, although that tends to be a personal preference, as are many other food tolerances.

One evening before a fifty-mile bicycle race in New York City, a teammate, Ernie, and I stopped by a doughnut shop. We ate a doughnut or two and when we went to pay my receipt came out with a star, which entitled me to a dozen free doughnuts. We took them back to our hotel room. The race started at six o'clock the next morning and my breakfast was a half-dozen doughnuts. Ernie ate one. My race went well. At the finish, all I could think of was polishing off the remaining doughnuts. Our coach ran up to me with a look of dread on his face.

"Did you hear what happened to Ernie?" he demanded.

"What?"

"He had to be taken to the hospital in an ambulance!"

Fearful, I asked if he had been hurt in a crash, although I didn't remember one in our race.

"Worse than that. He ate a doughnut for breakfast and right after the start he cramped up badly. He's at the hospital getting his stomach pumped."

I didn't dare tell our coach what I had eaten. But that also was a valuable lesson in how some foods affect one person and don't bother another. As with your riding techniques, it is best to experiment with meals before the major ride you're planning. Find out what works for you and stick with it.

Cycling clothing is best to wear on a ride because the shorts are made so that the inside of your legs won't get chafed from the saddle, and the fabric won't bunch up in your crotch—the way cotton gym shorts will. The fabrics, often made of Lycra or a Lycra blend with cotton or another synthetic, draw moisture from the skin, allowing moisture to rise out of the skin and flow out for evaporation, which is a cooling process. Moreover, cycling clothing fits snugly, without constricting, to cut wind resistance.

Cycling clothing comes in vibrant colors—a definite advantage in traffic. Motorists tend to look for other cars in traffic. Bicycle riders are easily overlooked. Wearing a jersey and a helmet with a brightly colored cover makes for good preventive medicine.

Protect your skin by applying sunscreen to all exposed areas. Wear sunglasses to protect your eyes. When it's cloudy outside, wear clear eyewear to keep grime out of your eyes.

Some of the year, especially in July and August, Texas is as hot as Hades. Keep this in mind and dress for the weather. You'll be comfortable in cycling shorts and a short-sleeved jersey, which should have three pockets in the back to hold food like cookies, bananas, and an extra drinking bottle or two.

When the weather is cold, a long-sleeved jersey worn over your regular jersey will keep you comfortable until you put in some miles and warm up. The long-sleeved jersey can then be rolled up and fitted into the rear pocket of your remaining jersey. Long-sleeved jerseys come in wool that is soft and snug-fitting, as well as in Lycra with a fine mesh cotton lining.

It may be tempting to wear earphones and listen to rousing music, but leave that equipment at home. Our ears are cupped to hear sounds from the direction we face; sounds from behind tend to be ignored unless their source is bearing down on us. Cycling is a joy, but there are survival rules of the jungle that require paying attention—listening to the sounds of traffic, looking at the texture of pavement to avoid holes or possible debris, and looking to see where you are going. Avoid distractions and stay alert. Don't be like the boxer who was decked by the punch he never saw coming.

Recreational rides draw enormous numbers of like-minded cyclists—12,000 line up for the Hotter 'n Hell Hundred. Before signing up for an event like the Hotter 'n Hell you must be comfortable with having cyclists all around you, especially with the way riders pass one another for miles and miles during these rides. It takes seasoning to feel comfortable around other cyclists, especially at such close quarters. One way to become comfortable is to take part in group rides, with friends or a cycling club. In doing so, you will learn that it is easier to ride when "drafting" behind the person in front, who effectively pushes away the wind to reduce resistance. Most effective drafting occurs when you follow the rear wheel in front by about a wheel's diameter—closer if you can manage it. Again, riding in a group helps you become more comfortable with that.

Another way to become relaxed around other cyclists is to go out to a grassy lawn with a friend or two. Practice riding shoulder to shoulder, bumping elbows and shoulders. If you fall, you're on soft ground, which beats the pavement. Bumping shoulders and elbows helps you get accustomed to being jostled without feeling threatened.

Most falls can be prevented. But they happen, so don't let them spook you. Get back on your bike as soon as you can and resume riding. If you're suffering from road rash, scrub out the asphalt, grit, and other matter. Apply a dressing and change it often.

Bicycle riding attracts a lot of technical-oriented people who have natural inclinations to work with nuts and bolts, gear cables, and assorted bicycle parts. You have two choices. One is to find a good friend with a mechanical penchant who doesn't mind taking care of your bicycle in exchange for a dinner or perhaps something else. The other is to regularly keep your tires pumped to around 100 pounds of pressure; replace your chain every 3,000 miles (about twice a year for people who ride often); and when something rattles, loosens, or doesn't work right, to promptly take it to your friend or a bike shop and get it taken care of.

Ever since John Dunlop, an Irish chemist, invented the pneumatic tire a century ago, punctures have been a way of life. Carry a spare tube and a reliable frame pump. They are worth their weight—carrying the extra weight beats walking home.

Bicycles come equipped with either tubular tires or clinchers. Tubulars are most often used for racing. They have the tube sewn into the tire, which is glued to the rim. Clinchers are also called wire-ons. They have a wire inside the bead of the tire which fits over (clinches) the tube and rests on the rim. Clinchers used to be considerably heavier than the tubulars, which can weigh as little as four ounces with the tire and tube together, but in recent years clincher tires have come close to the lightness of most road-racing tires. Gianni Bugno of Italy won the 160-mile world professional road race in 1991 in Stuttgart, Germany, riding with clinchers, which has helped give them greater currency in the cycling market.

If you've got tubulars, which give a slightly softer ride than clinchers, and a tire goes flat, it's a matter of tearing the tire off the rim and replacing it with a spare. Repairing a tubular is more labor intensive. After locating the puncture site, cut the threads that stitch the tire together, remove the tube to patch the cut, then replace the tube and re-stitch the tire together. Pump it up and you're off again. With clinchers insert a plastic tire lever to pull the tire off the rim, pull out the punctured tube, and replace it with a new tube. Before inserting the new tube, however, be sure to check the inside of the tire casing with your fingertips for the shard of glass or thorn that pierced your tire and deflated your tube. The culprit may still be imbedded there and could give you another flat.

I prefer clinchers, even for racing, because they are easier to repair than tubulars and don't need re-gluing from time to time. Clinchers are also considerably less expensive than tubulars—typically costing less than half. A big advantage with clinchers is that I can carry a tube repair kit, which is about the size of a pack of cigarettes and contains three plastic tire levers, glue, and assorted tube patches. The French have a saying, *jamais deux sans trois,* which means trouble comes in threes. With my repair kit, I'm better prepared.

The standard among experienced cyclists is to carry a small bag that fits neatly and inconspicuously behind the saddle and fastens onto the bottom of the seat post. Mine carries a spare tube, a tube repair kit, and an Allen wrench set that folds up like a jackknife and fits most of my bicycle's doodads.

When detective writer Raymond Chandler was interviewed about his career and quizzed on his weapon of preference, he rejected recommendations for a snub-nosed pistol or rifle. He suggested, "A twenty-dollar bill." That is also what I suggest. Put a double sawbuck and some form of identification in your jersey pocket or in the bag behind your saddle. While the twenty may be a small investment, you don't have to spend it whimsically, and in case you're caught in a sudden rainstorm and need to take a bus or a taxi home, you're equipped.

The right shoes are also important. Cycling shoes have firm soles designed to transfer energy more efficiently to the pedals. Soft-soled running or baseball shoes tend to be uncomfortable because the pedal pushes through the sole. When Miji (for Mary Jane) Reoch of Dallas started her cycling career in the early 1970s, she had an expensive Masi bicycle that was handmade in Italy, which she rode with bowling shoes because that was all that was available. She went on to win nine national cycling championships and a silver medal in the world championships in Rocour, Belgium. Reoch may be the only cyclist in the world to set national records in bowling shoes—they deserve to be bronzed. Today the cycling shoe business has evolved into an industry all its own.

As with two kinds of tires, there are two basic kinds of shoes—those for clipless pedals and those for pedals with toe clips and straps. Clipless pedals were introduced in the mid-1980s by a French firm, Look, that took the ski bindings they made and put them on cycling shoes. Many other companies have followed their lead in the cycling shoe business. Clipless pedals work with a cleat on the bottom of the shoe that fastens with a click onto the pedal. The foot thus has a direct connection, via the shoe and cleat, to the pedal.

Because people vary widely in their anatomy (a majority have a leg-length discrepancy of about a quarter of an inch), and because some are prone to knee problems, they may want a "floating" pedal that revolves about fifteen degrees to give the knee flexibility.

The other pedals have the longstanding toe clips, made of spring steel (sometimes plastic) with leather (sometimes nylon) toe straps to hold the foot on the pedal. On the sole of the shoe is a cleat with a groove across the bottom that allows the cleat to clamp over a portion of the pedal. The effect is to keep your foot securely on the pedal.

As with many other matters in cycling, choosing clipless pedals or regular toe clips and straps is largely a personal preference. My experience is that clipless pedals are easier to work in traffic when intersections require you to frequently stop and wait with one foot on the ground. But I have several cycling friends who tried the clipless pedals and went back to their toe clips and straps. Again, it's a personal preference that is up to you.

With both the clipless and regular toe clips and straps, a cyclist's feet are firmly positioned on the pedals. Walking, however, is awkward in cycling shoes. The cleats angle the toes up, putting your weight on the heel, and are slick on wood or linoleum surfaces.

New shoes for recreational cyclists have become available with the surge in consumer demand for cycling. These new shoes, made by Shimano and Nike, have an indention in the sole for a clipless fitting. They give a cyclist the advantage of a good grip on the pedal when riding. Off the bike, such as when walking into a restaurant for a sandwich and beverage with friends, walking in these shoes is the same as in any conventional shoe.

For your hands, I recommend wearing soft-leather cycling gloves, even in the hottest of weather. Cycling gloves have fingers that cover only the first joint. They absorb road shock that travels up the handlebars. Many brands of cycling gloves are made with gel pockets that are sewn into the palm to reduce road shock. Some brands, including Pearl Izumi and Specialized, make gloves with a terry cloth strip over the thumb to let you wipe sweat from your eyes.

My interest in cycling has led to a fascination with the uses of the bicycle: the utility of transportation that is quiet and nonpolluting; a sport that is one of the biggest and most enriching across the globe; and an increasingly popular recreational activity for adults, groups, or individuals.

William Saroyan, the author who stoically rejected the 1939 Pulitzer Prize for his play, *The Time of Your Life*, was a recreational cyclist. He grew up in Fresno, California, where he chose to set one of his most successful novels, *The Human Comedy*, which features a bicycle messenger. Saroyan had a stormy personal life, but the bicycle gave him a release from his compulsive gambling, unhappy marriage, and troubled relationship with his children. He once declared, "The bicycle is the noblest invention of mankind." Who can argue with that?

Since riding into that garage and falling over, my experiences have confirmed Saroyan's declaration. I've had the wonderful experience of riding with people like Martin and Valerie Meletio and Miji Reoch, whom I otherwise wouldn't have met, and have had the excuse— which I took advantage of—to travel to most of the country's big cities and countless small towns. Like other cyclists, I have learned the contours of the country on a bicycle, as Hemingway put it. My cycling went all right once I got past that garage.

INTRODUCTION

• • •

Ed Swan

 Much of Texas lives up to its vaunted reputation. It is true, however, that most of that elevated reputation was initiated and propagated by Texans them-selves. But, believe it or not, a great deal about the Lone Star state is even bigger than the legends.

Bicycle riding and touring in Texas is no exception. Texas is a great state to ride in. Whether it is the unbelievable number of quiet roads, the tastebud-blasting food, the big-hearted and broad-grinning folks, or the grand land itself, you have to ride Texas to appreciate it.

Very few other states or places in the world offer the diversity that Texas does. It may take a few miles (the Race Across America, with its 7- to 8-day winning times, takes almost half of that period to traverse Texas), but you can go from mountains to desert, to grassy plains, to rolling cedar-clad hills, to pine forests, to marshes with wild orchids, and back to plains and still be in Texas.

Whether you are traversing the Panhandle, Big Bend, the Llano Esta-cado, the Rio Grande Valley, the Coastal Plains, the Pineywoods, the Cross Timbers, the Hill Country, the Highland Lakes, or the Big Thicket—all of which are only some of Texas' distinct geographic areas—you will know you are in someplace special. Pick rides that take you across three or four of these different regions and you will know you are in the geographic patchwork quilt known as Texas.

You won't be alone either. There has been no official tally of the number of active Texas cyclists but they are often seen along the roadside in numbers as plentiful as bluebonnets in spring. There are almost 300 paid and pledge events a year around the state, including rallies, rides, centuries, weekend tours, and the like, making Texas a leader in cycling activity. The Hotter 'n Hell Hundred, held in Wichita Falls every August, draws around 12,000 riders, making it the most-attended one-day century in the country. The Texas Bicycle Coalition, an advocacy group, grew to more than one thousand members in its first year (1990), making it the largest statewide advocacy cycling organization in the country—and it's still growing.

Every major city sports one or more bike clubs (see the Appendices). When in the larger cities, I encourage you to contact the local group to find out where to ride and when other riders will be about. Circumstances change so much near population centers, it's best to get up-to-date information on metropolitan routes from the people who know.

This book focuses on the country, out in the hinterlands, where the quiet solace of the wide open spaces beckons. There are some loop tours, some town-to-town tours that loop back, and some point-A-to-point-B trips. While *Cycling Texas* will take you all over the state's back roads, we do not pretend to have covered all the places to ride. Some of these routes were chosen because no other book has featured them and others are just our handpicked favorites.

Texas has always drawn cyclists and other recreationalists. The state government's wildflower planting program yields more varieties of springtime wildflowers than you will see in any other state in the Union. Texas' wildness and untamed wilderness, some of which you can still sample, called to generations of *Texians*, as they were called in the beginning. Texans are proud of the fact that they were a separate nation prior to statehood. When Davy Crockett left Tennessee, upon the collapse of a checkered political career, he declared, "You can all go to Hell. I'm going to Texas!" There are still plenty of fiercely proud Texans who maintain the spirit behind that sentiment.

Ask a Texan what makes cycling in Texas so great and he or she will probably mention the roads. Considering that the state of Texas does not maintain roads within any incorporated town or city and that they leave many inner-county roads to the maintenance of the county itself, it is even more impressive that the Texas Department of Transportation maintains more than 76,000 miles of road. Over 40,000 miles of that total provide some of the most delicious riding experiences you will ever have—the Texas farm-to-market (FM) or ranch-to-market roads.

These pristine avenues seldom have shoulders but usually have very little traffic. They were built in a time when the state had coffers full of oil money and believed that if you had a place, any size of a place, and another place, you should build a very nice road from one to the other. The concept was to provide a way for farmers and ranchers to transport their goods to the markets in town, but they are now your quickest way to cycling nirvana. The web of FM roads allows most travelers to get from one town to another, usually avoiding any federal or state highways along the way. In his book, *Texas*, James A. Michener called them, "a network of rural roads equaled in few states." These roads are the heart of the routes in this book.

In spite of the fact a common culinary phrase in Texas is, "deep fry that sucker," you can get healthy food, that will burn you coming and going and that never stops, in almost any café. Tex-Mex is more than a style, it's a way of life. Want to break away from a pack of Texan hammer-heads? Just ask where to get the best Tex-Mex food or barbeque (or just whether hickory or mesquite is better cooking wood for barbeque bris-ket) and then ride like hell while they argue for hours. Imagine a menu where everyone eats like there will be no tomorrow and no bathroom scales and you have Texas cuisine.

Dogs are dogs everywhere. In Texas, the one-brown-eye, one-gray-eye, spotted Australian blue heeler is the breed to watch out for. They are bred to pen cattle by nipping at the dogies' heels. The same precautions that apply to dogs exist everywhere but, remember, many of these out in the Texas countryside are intended to scare away unwanted company. Watch your heels, but also make sure that they don't scare you into hurting yourself when they would never really do anything other than try to pen you.

Another real joy of cycling in Texas is the people. They will give you the shirts off their backs—no exaggeration. However, Texas still has a way to go in the cycling awareness and acceptance category. Texas drivers are just now getting used to cyclists on the roads, but many do not like the situation. Once, upon entering a theater in New York City, I saw two verbal opponents cursing each other. When I came out, they were still going at it. In Texas, one or two words and quicker than you could say "Whut?," things would have been resolved with action one way or another. In the same respect drivers will not tolerate a lot of verbal abuse or gesticulating before taking drastic action. Things are changing, thanks to advocacy organizations like the Texas Bicycle Coalition, but there is still a ways to go. So, guard yourself and don't get into any situation you cannot get yourself out of. Think about the next rider down the road, who could be the recipient of the wrath you provoke—it could be me.

On the other hand, Texas folks approach traveling cyclists with the same level of intensity. They will tell you their opinions, ask you questions that would make you blush even if posed by your spouse and then insist you take their assistance, all in the time it takes to hog-tie a calf. These are a backslapping people who are in love with life and not afraid to show it. Texans are the only cyclists I have ridden with that all, men and women, young and old, whoop and holler like ranchhands as they go down every steep hill. This is just not that common in New England.

Don't let the talk about precautions spook you. You are in for a real treat. If you are a Texan, you are about to encounter new roads and adventures that you never would have found without the help of this book. If you are one of *them*, a non-Texan, just cross the border and yore one of us. Before too long, you will be riding, whooping and hollering, and telling your companions in the oddest drawl, "Y'all come on!"

Welcome to the Lone Star state of mind . . . .

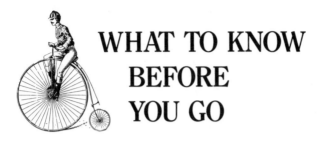

WHAT TO KNOW BEFORE YOU GO

Survey the Weather

Texas is popular with cyclists for more than just its well-maintained roads; cycling-friendly weather makes it a year-round playground. Fall comes late in Texas, usually arriving with October, and is slow to leave. Winter, too, makes a later appearance, and is most felt in January and February, when temperatures range on the average from high 20s to high 60s. Spring, with its abundant wildflowers and mild temperatures, brings delightful cycling conditions that last from March through mid-May. Summer stretches from mid-May to mid-September, delivering day after day of clear blue skies. However, Texas summers are to be respected. Temperatures can exceed 100 degrees and humidity levels often top 90 percent. Even cycling veterans find the heat and humidity taxing and proceed on summer rides with caution and plenty of water and sunscreen.

Be sure to study the average temperatures carefully and, regardless of the season, pay special attention to thunderstorm warnings. Texas rains are often so fierce that they are next to impossible and unsafe (due to flooding and loss of visibility) to ride in.

To obtain more specific up-to-date weather information, contact the following agency for the area you plan to explore:

BIG BEND COUNTRY
Big Bend Area Travel Association
P.O. Box 401
Alpine, Texas 79831
(915) 837-2326

EAST TEXAS
East Texas Tourism Association
P.O. Box 1592
Longview, Texas 75696
(214) 757-4444

HILL COUNTRY
Hill Country Tourism Association
1001 Junction Highway
Kerrville, Texas 78208
(210) 895-5000

NORTH TEXAS
Dallas/Fort Worth Area Tourism
    Council
P.O.Box 836167
Richardson, Texas 75083
(214) 234-4448

SOUTH TEXAS

Corpus Christi Area Convention
    and Tourist Bureau
1201 North Shoreline
P.O. Box 2664
Corpus Christi, Texas 78403
(512) 882-5603
1-800-678-6232

Brownsville Chamber of Commerce
650 FM 802
P.O. Box 4697
Brownsville, Texas 78523
(210) 546-3721
1-800-626-2639

NOTE: In South Texas weather can be very different on the coast and inland. If riding along the coast, call the Corpus Christi office; if riding inland, call the Brownsville office.

TEXAS PANHANDLE

Amarillo Convention and Visitor's
    Center
1000 Polk Street
P.O. Drawer 9480
Amarillo, Texas 70195
(806) 374-1497
1-800-692-1338 (TX)
1-800-654-1902

Lubbock Visitor's Convention
    Bureau
P.O. Box 561
Lubbock, Texas 79408
(806) 747-5232
1-800-692-4035 (TX)

NOTE: The north and south regions of the Panhandle experience such different temperatures that you will need to call separate sources for weather information. If riding north of Plainview, call the Amarillo office; if riding south of Plainview, call the Lubbock office.

Route Maps

Some cyclists prefer to create basic direction sheets, or route maps, to follow on rides. Route maps list only the basic directional information and should be drafted with quick reference in mind. A route map can be created for any of the rides in this book. Simply follow this sample, which is the route map for the New Braunfels Day Ride:

Direction	Road	Miles on Road
1. Head South	on San Antonio	1.3
2. Veer right	on Old San Antonio	1.3
3. Left	on Loop 337	0.3
4. Right	on FM 482 (at I-35 South)	4.8
5. Right	on Old Nacogdoches Road	3.0
6. Straight	onto FM 2252	2.0
7. Right	on FM 3009 (to cave turnoff)	5.7
8. Continue to cave and add mileage for cave excursion		1.6
9. Left	on 3009 (after cave)	2.4
10. Left	on FM 1863 West	6.7
11. Right	on Smithson Valley Road	6.0
12. Straight	onto FM 3159	6.4
13. Right	on FM 2673	6.0
14. Right	on River Road	12.0
15. Left	at T intersection, continue on River Road	1.2
16. Left	on Rock Street	1.0
17. Straight	onto Gruene Road to Gruene	0.8
18. Continue	on Gruene Road (after Gruene)	1.2
19. Right	on Common Street	1.4
20. Left	on Union Street	0.1
21. Right	on San Antonio	0.6

Mapping Out Rural Routes

Although this book has all the basic information you need to complete these rides, you should always consult as many maps as possible before setting out. Turn to the resource section at the back of the book to find map sources that are especially useful for riding in Texas.

While Texas' rural roads provide the solitude that cyclists crave, their remoteness can become unnerving when ridden without trustworthy maps in hand. Texas' rural roads are identified by a number and one of several names, including: Farm-to-Market (FM), Ranch-to-Market (RM), Farm Road (FR), and Ranch Road (RR). It is not uncommon for a rural road to be posted as an FM on one stretch and as an RM on another. These initials are interchangeable in all cases; however, you can always count on a rural road's assigned number to stay the same. One source, *The Roads of Texas* (Shearer Publishing, 1988) is the most comprehensive collection of road maps available and will be an invaluable reference to veteran and novice alike.

BIG BEND COUNTRY

• • •

George Sevra

 Geologic wonders dominate this mountain and desert landscape, from the earliest reef formations, laid down over 250 million years ago, to "modern" volcanic activity. The area is notable for its uncounted canyons that seem to appear from nothingness as you travel the back country. The best, and most, mountains in Texas rise high above the Chihuahuan Desert, from 4,000 feet to 8,000 feet in elevation.

Some of the best birding in Texas is found in the **Big Bend**—especially for those looking for raptors. Peregrine falcons are making a strong comeback in Big Bend, as well as numerous species of hawks, eagles, and owls. Other critters to watch for include mule deer, javelina, turkey, jackrabbits, dove, and quail. And of course, big, hairy tarantulas. These little furballs are best seen in October and November when they are actively seeking mates. They are harmless, if not provoked, and will crawl into your hand, which is a rather unique sensation.

Human habitation encompasses prehistoric Indians, the Spanish explorers, settlers, mercury miners, and modern ranchers. Terlinqua and Shafter ghost towns are reminders of man's lust for money at the expense of the environment and without regard for the future.

The Big Bend is a harsh land, often unforgiving to the unwary traveler. ***Do not*** **underestimate your need for water.** But, for the intrepid, well-prepared cyclist, this is the most rewarding cycling experience in Texas. Go for it!

Balmorhea
State Park Loop

Balmorhea State Park is located on U.S. 290, south of I-10. Located 4 miles south of the town of **Balmorhea,** the park was created by the Civilian Conservation Corps in the mid-1930s. The park was built around the **San Solomon Springs,** which created the world's largest spring-fed swimming pool. Crystal clear water, 30-foot depth, 1¾ acres, constant temperatures in the mid-70s, and varied marine life make a unique opportunity not only for swimmers, but also for scuba divers. The park is open 7 days a week, year-round, but the pool is only open to the public from the fourth Friday in May through Labor Day. There are numerous campsites and shelters available in the park as well as the **San Solomon Springs Court Motel.** Reservations are recommended well in advance during the peak season when the pool is open. Wildlife photography is very popular in the park, with an abundance of deer, javelina, hawks, roadrunners, and squirrels. And don't forget the fish in the pool. This is truly a worthy beginning to your exploration of the **Davis Mountains** and Big Bend Country.

This ride is an out-and-back (O.A.B.), beginning at the park entrance. Ordinarily, I don't like O.A.B.s, but this is a two-character ride. The park is at an elevation of 2,600 feet, **Fort Davis** is nearly 5,000 feet. You do the math . . . .

The extra bonuses of this ride are the options it presents. If you can arrange a shuttle, drive to Fort Davis and ride back, downhill. A short option is from Fort Davis to the summit of **Wild Rose Pass** and back to Fort Davis, a distance of 25 miles round trip. And if you must do more, take the 22-mile round trip side trip to the **Buffalo Trail Scout**

- **Starting point:** Balmorhea State Park (O.A.B.)
- **Mileage:** 64.5 miles (or more or less with options)
- **Terrain:** hilly and some flat
- **Best time to ride:** early spring to late fall
- **Traffic conditions:** very light to none
- **Road conditions:** good

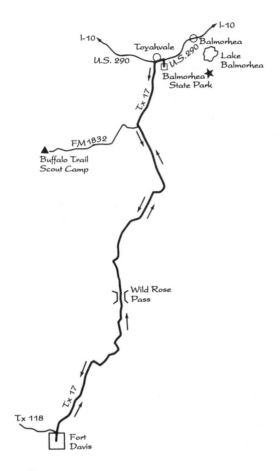

Camp. Regardless of which choice you make, as always in this region, take your time and don't forget to look back at the top of every climb. There is usually a pretty good view, and you earned it!

Hang a left as you exit the park and pass the **Hitchin' Post Cafe** on the right. Just 200 yards farther is the split of U.S. 290 and TX 17. Follow TX 17 to the left and don't look ahead. It's a good ways before you climb out of sight of **Toyahvale** and **Madera Valley.** When you top the first pass, about 5 miles out, look behind you. A sweeping vista of Madera Valley presents itself at your feet. This view gives you an idea of the climbing you have already done.

Another 1.5 miles to the top of the next pass and the road sweeps down and around through a narrower mountain valley. Enjoy this ¾-mile downhill, it's another 5 miles to the next one.

At the bottom of this refreshing descent is the junction of FM 1832 to the right. This is the Buffalo Trail Scout Camp side trip. If you have extra time, make this park-to-camp O.A.B. ride one day and Fort

Davis O.A.B. the next. It is a gorgeous ride through a narrow mountain valley—and certainly worth the effort.

The road begins a long, winding ascent, clinging to the west side of the narrow valley. Lush pastures and ponds, dotted with horses, cows, and maybe a mule deer follow you up the steep valley. The **Barrilla Mountains,** on the left, seem to mock your efforts as you pass the aptly named **Little Hell Tank.**

All good hills must end, and so does this one. This is a good place to take a break, look back and admire your handiwork, and devour a Power Bar. A breather from the climbing follows, with gentle downs, ups, and some flats marking the next half-dozen or so miles.

As the climbing begins again, **Wild Rose Pass Ranch** comes into view to your left, with its ornate entrance gate. The steepest section of the climb to Wild Rose Pass is about ¾ of a mile. At the summit (elevation 4,546 feet) is a historical marker. Reading these markers is a great excuse to rest, untangle your tongue from the spokes, and get ready for the next effort. In this case, it will be a rushing downhill for nearly a mile, followed by a flat runout to the first of three picnic areas. This marks the beginning of **Limpia Canyon.** It's uphill the rest of the way, but the scenery in the canyon is so spectacular, you hardly notice. The next 10.4 miles follow a curving, upward progression along **Limpia Creek,** past weathered spires, balanced rocks, and other spectacular formations of columnar basalt.

Five miles past the last picnic area, and only 3 miles from Fort Davis, is a remarkable rock fence on the right. The fence follows the road for .7 miles before turning off across the pasture. The end of the rock fence leaves just 2.5 miles to the junction of TX 17 and TX 118. Fort Davis begins to the left.

After a suitable rest period and some food, the ride back is great—it's 11-plus miles, all downhill to Wild Rose Pass. Up and over into the flats, it's a steady climb to the 20-mile mark and the top of the narrow, steep valley. The Barrilla Mountains, now on your right, no longer seem as intimidating as you fly down the valley to the scout camp junction. Then you have a short steep climb, a break, and the last climb to the Madera Valley vista. The last 5 miles to Toyahvale takes about 15 minutes. Once you're back in Balmorhea State Park, that oversized aquarium looks mighty inviting.

ACCOMMODATIONS: The Country Inn, on Highway 17, Balmorhea, (915) 375-2477.

CAMPING: Balmorhea State Park, on U.S. 290, south of I-10 (4 miles south of Balmorhea), (915) 375-2370.

Fort Davis
Scenic Loop

Fort Davis is the highest town in Texas at 4,900 feet. A notable point of interest is **Old Fort Davis National Historic Site.** This was an important outpost from 1854 to 1891 because it provided protection for the El Paso Road and Butterfield Overland Trail. This was also Apache and Comanche territory.

Other attractions along this route are **McDonald Observatory** atop **Mt. Locke** (6,791 feet elevation), the **Overland Trail Museum,** and the **Chihuahuan Desert Research Center.** This loop is the premier cycling tour for roadies in the entire state. Riding through the Davis Mountains, it is hard to remember you are still in Texas.

Begin the tour at any point in downtown Fort Davis and ride north toward the **Old Fort.** At the junction, past the fort, stay left on TX 118 and climb along Limpia Creek through Limpia Canyon. Although it is the same TX 118/TX 17 junction you take to Balmorhea, you will head in the opposite direction and climb into the real mountains.

The entrance to **Davis Mountains State Park** is 2.8 miles past the junction. The park contains another monument to the Civilian Conservation Corps of the '30s, **Indian Lodge.** It is styled after southwestern pueblos and has walls that are more than 18 inches thick. The park is also a favorite with bird watchers, being the only location in Texas that attracts the Montezuma quail.

The **Prude Ranch,** about 1½ miles farther, is a working dude ranch and resort. The Prude Ranch's calendar is full of all types of camps and special events. Included is the very popular Cyclefest in May,

- **Starting point:** Fort Davis (loop)
- **Mileage:** 74 miles
- **Terrain:** mountainous to gently rolling
- **Best time to ride:** October and November and March through May
- **Traffic conditions:** no traffic
- **Road conditions:** good

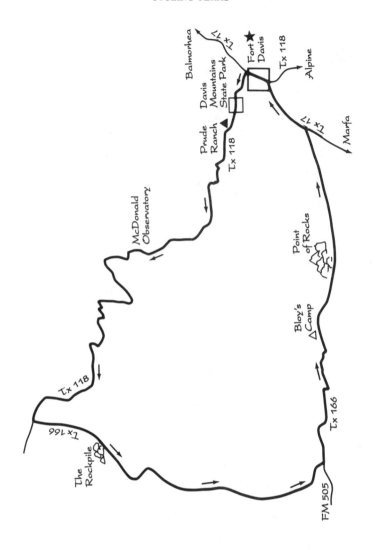

an event that includes several road races, tours, and mountain biking opportunities.

The climbing you have already done has taken you over the mile-high point and you will be there for the next 34 miles. The road appears to go straight into a wall, turning 90 degrees to the left. This elbow is the head end of **Deadman's Canyon,** which drops away to the left. It seems appropriately named at this point in the ride. The good news is you're one-half mile from the visitor center. The other good news is, you've got 60-plus miles to go . . . .

The **McDonald Observatory Visitor Center** (6,185 feet elevation) is a welcome sight, indeed. It is very important that you stop here. You *must* refill all water, even if you *think* you have enough. There are no reliable water sources for the next 60 miles once you leave the area. Rest and rehydrate while enjoying the great exhibits in the visitor center.

The ride up to McDonald Observatory and the summit of Mt. Locke are on the steepest paved gradient (17 percent) and highest paved road (6,791 feet elevation) in Texas. It is 2 miles up and 2 minutes down. The tour of the observatory and gonzo ride down will have you charged and ready for the next challenge on this loop. Refill your water before continuing.

The road continues straight, bends left and rolls into a sweeping right turn. You drop into **Brown's Canyon** (5,840 feet elevation) and immediately begin a 1¾-mile climb, gaining nearly 280 feet to the crest of **Fisher Hill** (6,119 feet elevation).

Stop before descending. Make sure you are in control, because the next mile drops more than 300 feet with a hairpin curve (to the left) just around the top bend. Try not to get carried away on this descent or you just might *get* carried away. This yah-hoo stretch has taken you into **Madera Canyon.** Madera Canyon (5,802 feet elevation) is filled with pine trees and has a lovely, peaceful picnic area. The word canyon usually denotes two things: (1) Something very beautiful and (2) something very difficult to climb out of. It will take just over a mile of thigh-burning effort to gain the 300-plus feet in elevation necessary to reach the top of **Beef Pasture Gap** (6,135 feet elevation).

From here, you begin to drop into the open plains ahead. That's right—you're now going *downhill.* The junction with TX 166 comes quickly and offers a great place to look back into the mountains. It is a truly awesome thing you have done.

But don't get too cocky. After you make a left onto TX 166, the road begins a gentle climb up **Adobe Draw** to the **Rockpile.** The Rockpile was a marvelous picnic area, with granite boulders to climb over. Unfortunately, vandalism forced park officials to fence off the area to protect fragile Indian pictographs.

The road continues to grow a little steeper as you approach the spectacular **Sawtooth Mountains** (7,686 feet elevation). The top of **H O Hill** (6,212 feet elevation), on the western shoulder of the Sawtooth Mountains, is the last monster climb. Buckle your helmet, because the road descends more than 500 feet in elevation in about 1½ miles. From this point through the rest of the loop, the terrain becomes rolling to gently rolling. You are also just past the halfway mark. There once was a sign designating this as the point of no return. Like so many other things, it disappeared.

You are at a junction in the middle of nowhere, and seemingly going nowhere. FM 505 connects TX 166 with U.S. 90, making the distances from Fort Davis to Van Horn and from I-10 to El Paso shorter. It also makes the trip considerably easier as well, because the road is straighter and flatter than the alternative. The junction is also a milestone because once there, you've cracked the 50-mile mark.

The route begins a long, gentle climb into **Medley Draw**—a narrow, winding canyon that is very pleasurable riding. Even though you are gaining several hundred feet, you don't seem to notice as before. You will actually climb over 550 feet before beginning the gradual descent back to Fort Davis. Just as the road levels is **Bloys Camp Meeting,** an interdenominational retreat where meetings have been held in August for more than 80 years. Here you may find the first and only water available, but you will have to check for it when you get there, so don't count on it.

The road flattens, straightens, and enters the vast open rangelands. A few miles past the camp, the road touches the base of an isolated peak. Covering the side of this peak is a tremendous tumble of rocks. Where the rocks meet the road is a picnic area called **Point of Rocks.** It's all downhill from here.

When you reach the junction of TX 166 and TX 17 there's only 2.5 miles to Fort Davis. Back at the **Fort Davis Drugstore,** enjoy a real fountain drink and reminisce about what you just accomplished. It is a tour you will remember forever.

ACCOMMODATIONS: The Limpia Hotel (circa 1912), on the town square (on route 17), Fort Davis, (915) 426-3237 or 1-800-662-5517. **Old Texas Inn,** on Highway 17, Fort Davis, (915) 426-3118. **The Prude Ranch** (cabins, bunkhouse, and camping facilities), on Highway 118 (just west of Fort Davis), Fort Davis, (915) 426-3202 or 1-800-458-6232. **Davis Mountains State Park Indian Lodge,** 6 miles west of Fort Davis on Highway 118, Fort Davis, (915) 426-3254.

CAMPING: Davis Mountains State Park, 6 miles west of Fort Davis on Highway 118, Fort Davis, (915) 426-3337. **The Prude Ranch** (RV and camping facilities), on Highway 118 (just west of Fort Davis), Fort Davis, (915) 426-3202 or 1-800-458-6232.

FOR MORE INFORMATION: Fort Davis Chamber of Commerce, P.O. Box 378 (located in the Hotel Limpia's lobby), Fort Davis, Texas, 79734, (915) 426-3015.

Texas Alps Triangle Tour

This tour begins in **Alpine** (4,485 feet elevation) and connects the three county seats in the largest tri-county area in the state—Alpine in Brewster County, **Marfa** in Presidio County, and Fort Davis in Jeff Davis County. Brewster, the largest county, and Presidio Counties are each bigger than Rhode Island and Delaware combined! The loop will take you through canyons and grasslands, alpine meadows and mountain passes—and through the truly wide-open spaces of the **Marfa Flats.**

Alpine bills itself as the town tucked into the "Alps of Texas." Nestled in a high meadow, surrounded by peaks, it has that alpine appearance. Alpine is also the home of **Sul Ross State University,** the "cowboy college." Best known for its animal and range management sciences, it is also highly regarded for its geology department. Mc-Donald's is at the southwest corner of the university, where U.S. 90 becomes divided. The tour begins here.

Exit the north side onto U.S. 90 west, away from the university. The heaviest traffic you will encounter in the entire region will be while going through Alpine. However, it's not all that bad and there is plenty of room to ride.

The road re-merges to become two-way again and just when you thought you were out of town, the **Apache Trading Post,** a "must stop" for books, information, and the most complete selection of topographic maps in the region, pops up on your right.

Now you're on the way to Marfa, greeted with a long, steady climb. Before you disappear over the hump, be sure to look back. The

- **Starting point:** Alpine (loop)
- **Mileage:** 72.3 miles
- **Terrain:** hilly to flat
- **Best time to ride:** mid-spring to late fall
- **Traffic conditions:** light
- **Road conditions:** good

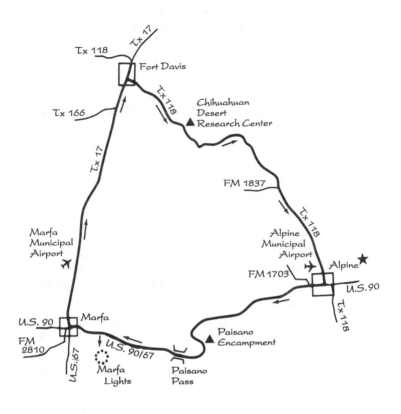

view explains why they call it Alpine. The double-summit peak on the left is called **Twin Sisters** (6,133 feet and 6,112 feet elevations).

The next 8 miles or so are the prettiest of this leg. Passing through high cliffs and meadows, the road carries you by the conical **Paisano Peak** (6,095 feet elevation) on the left. The railroad tracks join you for a spell and mark the beginning of a giant S curve. Parts of the old road are still visible on the left as you cross the Brewster-Presidio County line three times. Midway through the S, and still climbing, you will pass the **Paisano Encampment,** a Baptist retreat. Around the bottom of the S and the last crossing of the county line, you will begin the final ascent to **Paisano Pass** (5,125 feet elevation). An historical marker explains the origin of the pass's name and marks the halfway point to Marfa. From here it is a continuous, gentle descent into town. One important stop is about 4 miles past the pass, on the left. A rest stop and historical marker designate the prime viewing location for the mysterious **Marfa Lights.** These points of light appear frequently after sunset and their origins have yet to be explained.

The last 9 miles into Marfa are straightforward and mostly downhill. These wide-open prairie grasslands are part of the Marfa Flats. You will, certainly, see pronghorn antelope throughout this stretch, so keep your eyes peeled.

Marfa is best known for the Marfa Lights, but it also boasts the highest golf course in Texas and has the prettiest county courthouse in the triangle. At the stoplight and junction of U.S. 67 and TX 17, turn right on TX 17 toward the courthouse. A convenience store sits on the corner of this junction and is the best place to load up on Gatorade or your favorite fruit juice. Also, refill your water in Marfa because there won't be another chance for the next 21 miles, until you get to Fort Davis.

After making the turn toward the courthouse, on the left, is the **El Paisano Hotel.** The hotel was built in 1927 and was considered the finest accommodations between El Paso and San Antonio. In 1955 it was headquarters for cast and crew of the movie *Giant,* starring Rock Hudson, Elizabeth Taylor, and James Dean. Follow TX 17 around the right side of the courthouse and you will quickly leave Marfa behind.

TX 17 runs darn-near straight to Fort Davis. Twenty-one miles through open grasslands, full of pronghorns. About 4.5 miles out of town is the **Marfa Airport.** The road then continues a steady, gentle ascent to the top of a low pass about 12.5 miles out. From here, the valley ahead sprawls before you. The downhill takes you into the flats and straight into Fort Davis. Along this last stretch, McDonald Observatory can be seen in the Davis Mountains to the left.

The route joins TX 118 at the south end of town, next to the **Jeff Davis County Courthouse.** Take a break at the drugstore fountain, next block, on the left. After refreshing yourself and refilling your water bottles, head back to the junction and turn left onto TX 118 to Alpine.

Just $\frac{1}{2}$ mile out, you'll come across an historical marker. In the first couple of miles, watch for more pronghorns. A must-stop-and-look-back spot comes at the top of a hill at the 3.9-mile mark. Check out the beautiful valley with McDonald Observatory in the distance. Less than $\frac{1}{2}$ mile farther is the entrance to the Chihuahuan Desert Research Center. The visitor center is open from May 1 to Labor Day, from 1:00 P.M. to 5:00 P.M on weekdays and 9:00 A.M. to 6:00 P.M. on weekends. Hiking trails and a desert arboretum are open to those who want to see more.

Immediately past the center's entrance is the start of a great downhill—the best of the whole loop. After whizzing onto the flats, the road hugs the cliffs to your right and has open bottomland to your left.

These bottomlands are favorite gathering places for wild turkey, mule deer, and ducks.

The next 6 miles roll through scenic mountains. A refreshing downhill takes you to the junction with FM 1837 and also takes you out of the mountains. The houndstooth peak on your right is **Mitre Peak,** a well-known landmark. The road, from this junction, becomes gently rolling and predominantly downhill. Eight miles of grasslands (watch for pronghorns) carry you to the **Alpine-Caspares Airport** and the edge of town. Two miles more is the junction with U.S. 90 and U.S. 67. Turn left (west) on U.S. 90 and McDonald's is less than a mile.

Back at McDonald's, sipping on a chocolate shake, you will have completed the easiest loop in this neck of the woods (or desert)— relatively speaking, of course.

ACCOMMODATIONS: Holland Hotel, 209 West Holland Avenue, Alpine, (915) 837-3455. The Chamber of Commerce can recommend additional hotels and motels in Alpine.

CAMPING: Pecan Grove (RV park), on U.S. 90, Alpine, (915) 837-7175.

FOR MORE INFORMATION: Alpine Chamber of Commerce, 106 North Third Street, Alpine, Texas, 79831, (915) 837-3638.

The Really
Big Loop

The Really Big Loop encompasses all the best of Big Bend Country: high prairies and higher mountains, some of the steepest climbs and fastest downhills, and one of the ten most scenic highways in the United States.

A tough four-day, or more comfortable five-day, trip of the best cycling in Texas, the Really Big Loop is not for the faint of heart. Those of you with the experience and willingness to accept the challenge will be rewarded with one of your life's greatest achievements: completing the Really Big Loop in Big Bend Country.

The description of this tour is in the form of a roadlog to better guide you to the major points of interest and so you will always know

- **Starting point:** Marfa (loop)
- **Route:** day one—Marfa to Marathon
  day two—Marathon to Study Butte (Big Bend National Park)
  day three—Study Butte to Lajitas
  day four—Lajitas to Presidio
  day five—Presidio to Marfa
- **Mileage:** day one—59.6 miles
  day two—97 miles (shorter w/options)
  day three—17 miles (longer if less than 97 miles completed on day two)
  day four—50 miles
  day five—62 miles
  total—285.6 miles
- **Terrain:** flat to mountainous
- **Best time to ride:** early to late spring, early fall to late winter (Do not attempt this ride during summer months.)
- **Traffic conditions:** moderately busy in Alpine, light to none elsewhere
- **Road conditions:** good

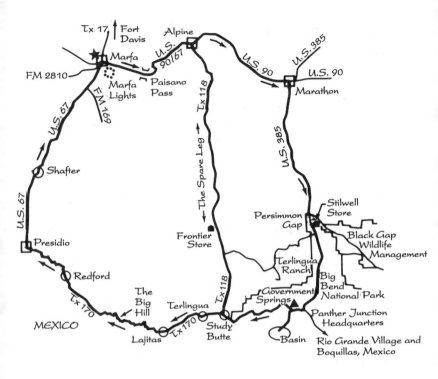

where you are and what is ahead of you. Out here the elements have a
decided advantage and you will need all the help you can get. As always,
take your time. Why rush through the breathtaking scenery when you
have all day for each leg? Watch for wildlife, look behind you at the top
of every hill, and enjoy the ride. And remember, drink, drink, drink!

DAY ONE: Marfa to Marathon

Marfa is the logical starting point because it offers the best
first-day and the best finishing stretch for the tour.

0 mile　　　　U.S. 90 and U.S. 67 converge in Marfa and head east
　　　　　　　together. You will start at their junction, following
　　　　　　　them east.

9.4 miles　　　Rest stop and historical marker for the Marfa Lights.
　　　　　　　The road has been climbing gently the whole way. It
　　　　　　　continues to climb in the miles ahead.

13.6 miles　　Summit of Paisano Pass and its historical marker. This
　　　　　　　is also the start of a long S curve, all downhill.

15.8 miles   Paisano Baptist Encampment and Paisano Peak loom above. You're ripping downhill here, but be sure to look at the peak and the scenery opposite the encampment.

19.2 miles   Around a corner, straight ahead is Twin Sisters Peak.

22 miles   You're at the top of the day's last climb. From here it's an easy, downhill roll into Alpine. This is an excellent vantage point to see why the area is called "the Alps of Texas."

25 miles   Apache Trading Post is on the left.

28 miles   Stop at the first stoplight by the train station. If you're looking for somewhere to stop for a lunch break, turn right, cross the tracks, take the next right, and one block down on the left is the **Little Mexico Café.**
Deli sandwiches are also available at the **Alpine Bakery,** which is two blocks past the first stoplight on the right. Be sure to fill your water bottles while you are stopped. Return to U.S. 90 and U.S. 67 East.

36.8 miles   The junction of U.S. 90 and U.S. 67 (where they split, U.S. 67 heading north and U.S. 90 continuing east) has a rest stop and historical marker. Continue straight on U.S. 90 to Marathon. The road appears to head into the distant **Glass Mountains.** Instead, it swings south around the tip, through a flat pass.

46 miles   Look left at the fabulous limestone reef uplift formation, some 250 million years old (give or take a week).

50.8 miles   Note the giant yucca on the right, visible for the past several miles. The flat-top mountain to the distant right is **Santiago Peak.** You will be seeing this peak until late into tomorrow's ride. Look ahead and follow the curve of the road, noticing the patch of green, which is Marathon, at the end. Notice, also, it is a nice, gentle downhill.

59.6 miles   You roll into Marathon, gateway to **Big Bend National Park.**

Marathon is the midway point between Fort Stockton and Big Bend on the Comanche War Trail. From 1840 to 1880, Comanches raided everything they found in the area. No one was safe until the United States Cavalry established **Fort Peña Colorado** in 1879. Today, the site is a public park, located 5 miles south on Post Road. It is well worth the 10-mile side trip.

DAY TWO: Marathon to Big Bend National Park

U.S. 385 turns south at the east end of Marathon. There is no water for the next 43 miles. You just seem to go and go and to be mostly alone as Santiago Peak slowly passes on the right. Although this stretch is not particularly challenging physically, it is mentally strenuous as you slip past the **Woods Hollow Mountains** and the **Tinaja Mountains** on your left. At the base of the **Santiago Mountains,** you finally arrive at the entrance to Big Bend National Park and the start of the climb through **Persimmon Gap.**

0 mile   Junction U.S. 90 and U.S. 385, turn right onto U.S. 385 toward Big Bend National Park.

5.6 miles   United States border patrol check point, where north-bound traffic is checked. The road continues to be long and gently rolling.

8.8 miles   Notice the remarkable geologic formations called "flatirons" to your right.

10.7 miles   Sign identifying **Horse Mountain** (5,012 feet elevation) to the left.

11.2 miles   Rest area and historical marker explaining some of the area's unique geology.

24.5 miles   Sign identifying Santiago Peak (6,521 feet elevation) to the right. The road continues to be rolling to gently rolling.

27 miles   Around the corner is the first view of the **Chisos Mountains** in the far distance.

37 miles   Historical marker at **Double Mills.** If anyone happens to be here, water may be available but don't count on it.

40.5 miles Junction with FM 2627, (on your left) to the **Stillwell Store** (6 miles) and **La Linda,** Mexico (26 miles).

41.6 miles Entrance to Big Bend National Park. Start the climb through Persimmon Gap. Within the park, all paved roads have markers every mile. The numbers descend as you approach **Panther Junction,** the park's headquarters. These mile markers are used for easiest reference while in the park. Cumulative mileage will be shown in parenthesis.

27 miles
(42.8 miles) Persimmon Gap is nearest the 27 mile marker, as is the **Persimmon Gap Ranger Station.** Interrupt the downhill to stop at the station and refill water bottles. The next water is 27 miles away, most of which is uphill.

23+ miles
(47.7 miles) A dirt road to the right leads to **North Rosillos Ranch** and **Terlingua Ranch.** This road connects with TX 118, the Spare Leg route, and is not suitable for road bikes.

13 miles
(57 miles) Dagger Flat Road is to the left. It is also a dirt road and is not suitable for road bikes.

8 miles
(62 miles) There is a fossil exhibit to the left. The road is paved for the 300 feet to the exhibit. Just beyond this junction is the bridge over **Upper Tornillo Creek.** Watch for javelina in the area. From this point it's uphill all the way to Panther Junction.

4 miles
(66 miles) **Hannold Spring and primitive camping area,** which allows tent camping only and prohibits fires. Walk up the short footpath to the grave and historical marker. Although we can only imagine life in those days, just standing on the spot gives you a special feeling.

0 mile
(70 miles) **Panther Junction headquarters.** Obtain permits and pay nominal entrance fee here, taking a break after the last 4 tough miles. Several options now present themselves. First, refill your water bottles; this is the best available water for the rest of the trip. Continue west toward the gas station.

.3 mile Gas station and convenience store on left. If you in-

(70.3 miles)   tend to camp outside the **Basin,** this is your only source for food. The road is downhill from Panther Junction for about a mile, then begins a steady 2-mile climb to the Basin junction. The Basin offers full services, including restaurant, lodge, camping, and store. There is also hiking and horseback riding.

3 miles   Junction with Basin Road. Here you will decide which
(73 miles)   way to continue.

Option One: It's a 5-mile *climb,* then a 2-mile descent into the Basin. If you have anything left, this chunk of asphalt equals the exhilaration of the ride to McDonald Observatory—maybe it's better, because this is the end to a long day's ride.

Option Two: Immediately past the Basin junction is the Grapevine Hills Road junction to the right. Turn right onto the dirt road and just one-quarter mile down, on the left, is **Government Springs primitive camping area,** a good place to stop for the night.

Option Three: What direction is the wind blowing? If there's an easterly wind, then the 24-mile ride to **Study Butte** (Study rhymes with Judy) is a breeze.

This is the longest and most challenging alternative to the end of day two's route. It can be extremely taxing, even for experienced cyclists. When I did this ride I had a south-southeast wind all day from **Marathon.** That's 70 miles of headwinds. After a brief rest at the gas station, and a quart of Gatorade, I made the climb to the Basin junction. My original intent was to camp at Government Springs, but the riding became so much fun after the junction, I couldn't quit. Two great downhills, some flats, a 10-percent grade downhill, a gently rolling downhill, and some 13 miles fell behind me. At the Ross Maxwell Scenic Highway junction, I rested, drank, and ate a Power Bar. This close to Study Butte, I decided to go for it. A fast downhill, a good but not difficult climb, and a gently descending stretch carried me to the Old Maverick Road junction. This used to be a ranger station at the west entrance.

You are now only one-half mile from the park entrance. But what a half mile! Does a 6-percent grade downhill sound fun to you? Yeah, it does to me too! A mile past the park sign, over one last little hump, and *poof*! . . . Study Butte. I did this 24-mile ride in one hour and ten minutes, fully loaded with gear. My normal touring pace is ten miles per hour. I mention this time because it works to illustrate the ease of doing this section with anything resembling a tailwind. Simply said, take the opportunity when the winds allow. The drawback is a 97-mile day before you camp.

Now that you are, literally, over the hump, the first sighting of refreshment is the **Study Butte Mall** on your right, but don't get too excited because that's just what the locals call it. A little over a mile farther is the junction with TX 170 to the left. Ignore everything else and turn here. About one-half mile downhill is a large bridge across **Terlingua Creek.** Immediately across the bridge, on the left, is **Big Bend Travel Park;** camp here. The **La Kiva Restaurant** is also here. Prepare your buds for the best barbeque chicken or beef in West Texas.

The Basin and Government Springs options create the 5-day tour and make Lajitas the stop for your next overnight. However, if you chose option three, you have two more choices. **Option 3A:** From Study Butte, continue on to **Lajitas** for a 17-mile ride. In Lajitas, take a raft trip on the Rio Grande with Big Bend River Tours, then stay overnight in the **Lajitas campground. Option 3B:** From Study Butte, continue on Highway 118 to FM 170 West. Turn left (west) toward **Presidio,** which is 67 miles away.

Anytime you undertake a trip of this length, the importance of pre-planning cannot be overstated.

DAY THREE: Study Butte to Lajitas

Now that I have thoroughly muddled your brain, we continue with the ride from the Study Butte junction of TX 170.

0 mile   At the TX 170 junction, turn left, opposite the Chevron station.

.5 mile   The **Terlingua Creek bridge.** Here you will start a steep climb followed by several deep dips. This mile-long stretch is potentially dangerous; use extra caution.

5 miles   Turnoff to **Terlingua ghost town.** The dirt road is easily rideable on a road bike. Stop into the **Terlingua Trading Post** and look at their marvelous selection of books on local, regional, and southwest history and folklore. They offer the best pickin's between San Antonio and El Paso. Return to TX 170 via the dirt road and continue toward Lajitas.

8 miles   **Pepper's Hill**—you'll know it when you see it. Once you top the hill, it is about an 800-feet elevation loss to Lajitas over the next 8.5 miles.

17 miles   **Lajitas on the Rio Grande,** which is actually a resort, not a town. It has four hotels/motels, one restaurant, and a bar—all of which are owned by the same corporation. There is also an RV park and a campground. The best food is across the Rio Grande in **Pasa Lajitas, Mexico,** at **Garcia's.** Ask for directions at **Big Bend River Tours** on the **Boardwalk. Desert Sports** bike shop offers guided mountain bike tours for those interested in exploring off-road trails.

DAY FOUR: Lajitas to Presidio

TX 170 from Lajitas to Presidio is better known as the River Road. The road closely parallels the **Rio Grande** and passes through breathtaking scenery. It has been named as one of the ten most scenic highways in the United States. It is breathtaking in other ways, as well. If any road can be called a roller coaster, this is it. Prepare yourself for the toughest stretch of pavement in Big Bend.

0 mile   Starting in Lajitas, the road to Presidio begins with a series of three dips that are just the precursor of things to come.

6.9 miles   The road curves, dips, climbs, and crosses the **Fresno Creek bridge** here. The main house for **Fresno Creek Ranch** is visible from the top of the hill past the bridge, back to your left.

9.9 miles   The **Grassy Banks campground.** It is part of the **Big Bend Ranch State Natural Area** and permits are required.

11.7 miles Note the rock formations in white volcanic tuff on the right.

12.3 miles **Madera Canyon campground and river access.** It is also part of the Big Bend Ranch State Natural Area and requires a permit.

13 miles **Tee Pees Rest Area.** Gather your wits here, the Big Hill starts around the next corner.

13.65 miles This point is the only break in the climb. The next one-half mile is a killer.

14.1 miles Summit of Big Hill. It's a 15-percent climb, followed by a downhill of equal proportion. Use caution! The curves do not allow you to just turn it loose. But, before you go rip-snortin' downhill, stop and check out the view. Ahead, visually follow the course of the river and it will lead you into **Colorado Canyon.** This canyon offers the best half-day raft trip. Check out the volcanic rock and the enormous rock slide, which is believed to have been caused by lightning.

20.8 miles **Closed Canyon** parking area. A short hike takes you into Closed Canyon, a very narrow, steep cut into the Colorado Canyon. This is also part of Big Bend Ranch State Natural Area, but no permit is required to hike into the canyon.

22.9 miles Colorado Canyon entrance and put-in area for raft trips.

27.2 miles Leaving the Big Bend Ranch State Natural Area. (Did someone say, "roller coaster?") You're past the point of no return now; it's just 8 miles to **Redford.**

35 miles Redford city limits.

36.3 miles **C Store,** where you can get fresh water and cold drinks. The road does not have quite as many curves, but it is still up and down. (I did this 50-mile stretch against a sustained 20-plus-mile-per-hour headwind with 35-mile-per-hour gusts!) Pray for a tailwind.

43.9 miles Casa Piedra Road sign to the right. This dirt road leads 26 miles to the **Big Bend Ranch headquarters.** This road is not suitable for road bikes.

45 miles Overhead cable car for gauge station on the Rio Grande.

48 miles   **Ft. Leaton State Historic Site,** a frontier Spanish mission, established in 1759. It was acquired by Ben Leaton, the area's first Anglo settler, in 1846 and is open daily from 8:00 A.M. to 4:30 P.M.

49 miles   Presidio city limits.

52 miles   Junction with U.S. 67. The tour turns right at this junction. One mile, straight ahead, is the international border crossing into **Ojinaga, Chihuahua, Mexico.** Not your typical tourist border town, Ojinaga is more laid back and is a good spot for dining and lodging. Presidio, located at "La Junta," the junction of the **Rio Conchos** of Mexico and the Rio Grande, is often the hottest spot in Texas and sometimes the hottest in the United States. This provides the biggest caution for not doing this ride in the summer.

DAY FIVE: Presidio to Marfa

You're almost there! This leg takes you through the **Chinati Mountains** and the **Cuesta del Burro Mountains,** past **Chinati Peak** and the old silver mining town of **Shafter.** There's still lots of climbing yet to do, but a grand reward awaits you . . . .

0 mile   Start out in Presidio, at the **Balia Inn.** Follow signs for U.S. 67 North. The first 2 miles are a steady climb.

5.2 miles   **Presidio International Airport.**

8.25 miles   A new convenience store has been built here. This is a good place to stop if you need anything you forgot to get in Presidio.

12 miles   The *real* climbing begins. Be sure to look back, often, at Ojinaga in the distance. It gives you a true perspective of how far you have already climbed.

15 miles   Last chance to steal another look back at Ojinaga.

16.7 miles   **Profile of Lincoln** sign.

18 miles   The first ruins of the **Shafter Mining District** appear to the left at the start of another steep climb. Just over the top of the hill on the left are the ruins and foundations of a processing plant. Numerous ruins are visible during the exhilarating downhill into Shafter.

19.5 miles   Entering Shafter, which is considered a ghost town. There is no store and the schoolhouse is for sale. Water is available at the post office behind the church.

19.8 miles   **Cibolo Creek.** You'll start another climb, followed by a good downhill and more climbing, before leaving the mountains.

25 miles   The start of a long, straight, rolling stretch. Here you leave the confines of the mountains and begin climbing open ridges.

26.6 miles   A border patrol inspection station, which is not always open. It's really just a few signs and a wide spot in the road.

27.2 miles   Sign identifying Chinati Peak (elevation 7,730 feet) to the left.

34 miles   Wide open, grassy, rolling hills. Back to your right are the Chisos Mountains. This is pronghorn country. Soon, you will see the road climb a monster ridge ahead. Take heart, it is the *last* climb of the tour. Be sure to look around and behind you as you ascend. The vistas are nothing less than spectacular.

38.5 miles   The top of **Childress Hill.** At the crest, take a moment and admire the scene laid out before you. From here, looking straight ahead, scan the horizon to the right. At one o'clock is **Cathedral Mountain,** at two o'clock is Santiago Peak and at three o'clock are the Chisos Mountains. If you look closely you'll see Marfa at eleven o'clock. (Drum roll, please.) It is at this point that you see the reward for all your hard work. The next 12 miles rip by in less than 30 minutes.

53.4 miles   Junction FM 169. This road turns to dirt and is not suitable for road bikes.

54.5 miles   You know you're getting close when you start seeing motel billboards. And, lo and behold, just over the rise and straight ahead is Marfa. And even better, with no major hills to battle, it's just a gentle roll into town.

56.7 miles   Another border patrol inspection station, where you must stop.

60 miles   Marfa city limits. There's an old World War II airbase to the left, which is now part of the **Chinati Foundation.** Watch for pronghorns in the green pastures to the right.

62 miles   Junction U.S. 67 and U.S. 90. Straight ahead the **Presidio County Courthouse** majestically dominates the cityscape.

All I can say about this tour is, "Wow!" As tough as parts of the route are, the finish comes too quickly. I consider this ride the best multi-day tour in Texas. Would I do it again? Believe it!

The Spare Leg: Alpine to Study Butte

This route is also very hilly to rolling and long. It takes you past mountains named **Ord, Cathedral, Cienaga,** and **Elephant;** through open desert scrublands; and, again, past mountains called **Packsaddle, Hen Egg, Wildhorse,** and **Bee.** It is a tough stretch of road that can be plugged in after day two's ride, or into another portion of the tour, producing varying loops within the Really Big Loop.

Load up on water, in bottles and your Camelbak (a water-drinking system). You will need all you can carry, because it is 55-plus miles to the next waterhole. Once again, I use a roadlog format for this leg's description. The remoteness of the area makes it imperative that you always have some idea of where you are and what is ahead and how far.

0 mile   The junction of U.S. 90 East and TX 118 South is toward the eastern end of Alpine and one block west of McDonald's. Head south and the road begins with a gentle rise.

5 miles   Start of the Alpine Big Hill—a 1.5-mile climb that is quite steep. Be sure to look back at the peaceful view of Alpine in the valley. The road continues very hilly.

10.5 miles   Sign identifying Mt. Ord (elevation 6,700 feet) to the left. As you come out of the big hills, Elephant Mountain and Santiago Peak come into view to the left. The terrain becomes less severe and more open.

14.2 miles   A Border Patrol Inspection station for northbound traffic.

16 miles   **Woodward Ranch.** Camping, mountain biking, and rock hunting for red agate are available here.

17.5 miles   Rest stop.

22.7 miles   Sign identifying Cienaga Mountain (elevation 6,580 feet), back over your right shoulder. Elephant Mountain looms on the left. Note the road switch-backing up the left side.

26 miles   Rest stop.

26.5 miles   Entrance to **Elephant Mountain Wildlife Management Area.** The road begins a very long, gently rolling stretch here.

28.8 miles   Sign identifying Elephant Mountain (elevation 6,230 feet). Try to avoid looking at the mileage signs. They can be very depressing.

34.3 miles   Litter barrels at the top of a ridge. The road goes on forever. The mountains ahead are the **Christmas Mountains** on Terlingua Ranch. I have dubbed the next 8 to 9 miles Raptor Alley. Especially in late fall, numerous species of hawks, eagles, and owls can usually be spotted along the roadside.

39 miles   The halfway point, opposite Santiago Peak on the left—it will seem like you are in the middle of nowhere.

41.6 miles   Sign identifying Santiago Peak (elevation 6,521 feet) to the left.

44.2 miles   This is the top of the ridge you saw from the litter barrels, 10 miles ago! The Chisos Mountains come into view here. **West Corazone Peak** is the houndstooth-top mountain in front of the Chisos.

49.8 miles   At the top of this steep ridge climb, a grand vista opens before you. To the left is **Nine-point Mesa,** and to the right is **East Corazone Peak** (houndstooth) and the rest of the Christmas Mountains. Behind these are the Chisos, with **Casa Grande** (the square peak) and **Emory Peak** (the highest) most prominent. Continuing to the right, the double-summit is Packsaddle and the next highest is Hen Egg. The large mesa is **Aqua Fria** and the continuing ridge line is part of the **Solitario** on Big Bend Ranch State Natural Area. Lastly, beyond the ridge in the far distance is **Sierra Rica,** a

9,000-foot peak in Mexico. Enjoy the nice downhill, while you can.

55.5 miles The **Frontier Store,** where cold refreshments, food, and camping are available. Refill your water here.

61.2 miles Entrance to Terlingua Ranch. This is the other end of the road within the national park, that turns off just below Persimmon Gap. Again, it is not suitable for road bikes.

65 miles **Longhorn Motel.**

67.5 miles Very steep hill begins. Steep grades up and down for the next 10 miles.

71.8 miles **Wildhorse Station,** store, and cabins.

76.5 miles Great finishing descent from the shoulder of Bee Mountain into Study Butte.

78 miles Junction TX 118 and TX 170. Continue straight to enter the park or turn right to go to Lajitas and Presidio. I told you it was tough.

ACCOMMODATIONS: Holiday Capri/Thunderbird Motel, 509 West U.S. 90 (west of U.S. 67 junction), Marfa, (915) 729-4326 or (915) 729-4391. **The Gage Hotel** (a restored historic landmark, circa 1927, P.O. Box 46, Marathon, (915) 386-4205. **Marathon Motel** (west end of town on U.S. 90), Marathon, (915) 386-4241. **Easter Egg Valley Motel,** P.O. Box 228 (just before Terlingua Creek bridge), Terlingua, (915) 371-2430 or (915) 371-2254. All reservations for Lajitas should be made through the **Badlands Hotel;** call them at 1-800-527-4078. **Balia Inn,** north of town on U.S. 67, Presidio, (915) 229-3211.

CAMPING: Marathon Motel (also has RV and tent camping), on the west end of town on U.S. 90, (915) 386-4241. **Southern Route Cafe & RV Park** (also allows tent camping), 410 Highway 90 East, Marathon, (915) 386-4512. **Big Bend Travel Park** (TX 180 at Terlingua Creek), Study Butte, (915) 371-2251.

FOR MORE INFORMATION: Alpine Chamber of Commerce, 106 North Third Street, Alpine, Texas, 79831, (915) 837-3638.

LOCAL BIKE SHOPS: Desert Sports, P.O. Box 584 (at Lajitas on the Rio Grande), Terlingua, (915) 424-3366 or 1-800-523-8170.

THE BACKWOODS OF EAST TEXAS

• • •

Ann K. Baird

To either the first-time visitor or the uninitiated native, East Texas is full of surprises. With its verdant thickets, moss-draped cypresses, and dense pine forests, East Texas has more in common with the deep South than it does with the rest of Texas—another example of the state's striking diversity.

Even more surprising to those who think Texas history begins and ends with the Alamo, is that the site of the earliest human settlements in the state is in East Texas. From the prehistoric Caddo villages to the Spanish missions and trading posts to the pioneer colonies from Missouri, Kentucky, and Tennessee, East Texas has a rich, far-reaching history. Today, it boasts a number of historical parks, homes, museums, and cemeteries that chronicle its roots.

In places, East Texas seems as isolated as the western parts of the state. There are four national forests and a national preserve here, and the roads meander through them for 20 or 30 miles without a sign, store, or gas station. This can be a bit problematic if you're like me and like to munch as much as you like to pedal. But if you enjoy miles of lightly traveled roads shaded from the merciless Texas sun, you'll find East Texas an unexpected cycling delight.

The Origins
of Texas Tour

This loop, beginning and ending in **Palestine,** is a wonderful way to experience the history and scenery of East Texas. This loop extends as far as the historic city of **Nacogdoches** and ends with a ride on the **Texas State Railroad** from **Rusk** back to Palestine. The train runs on a turn-of-the-century steam-powered Iron Horse locomotive, and the two connecting depots in Rusk and Palestine reflect the architecture of the original train stations in the area.

To complete the entire loop you should be prepared to carry enough clothing and other items on your bicycle for three days of riding and two overnight stays. If you prefer not to carry so much gear, directions for shortened versions of this loop follow.

A beautiful time to tour this area would be during dogwood season, from late March to early April, when the prolific native dogwood trees blossom. But if you visit during this time, expect increased crowds and traffic, which may compromise your enjoyment. Also, make accommodation and train reservations well in advance, because the ride is a popular dogwood-viewing activity.

- **Starting point:** Palestine (loop)
- **Route:** day one—Palestine to Alto
    day two—Alto to Nacogdoches
    day three—Nacogdoches to Rusk (ride train back to Palestine)
- **Mileage:** day one—35 miles (or 61.5 miles with options)
    day two—27 miles
    day three—38 miles
    total—100 miles (more or less with options)
- **Terrain:** rolling with a few short, steep climbs
- **Best time to ride:** March and April, and the fall
- **Traffic conditions:** very light
- **Road conditions:** good

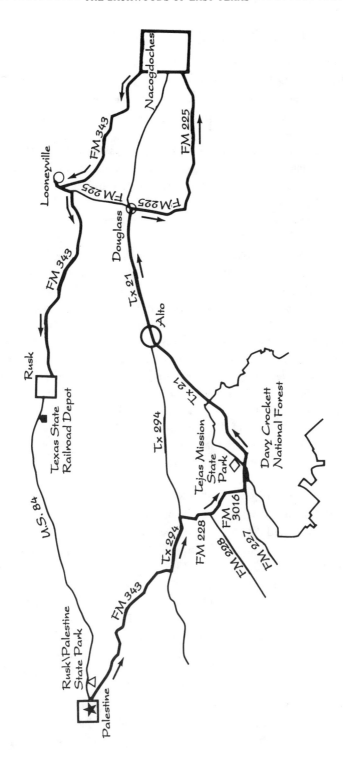

DAY ONE: Palestine to Alto

Although the recommended starting point for this tour is **Palestine State Park,** where you'll return on the train, don't neglect the city of Palestine (pronounce it Palace-steen if you don't want to be labeled a Yankee spy). Your first stop might be the **Palestine Convention and Visitors Bureau,** at 502 North Queen Street for a city map and brochures on the local attractions. If you're visiting on the weekend go to the building's basement, where maps and brochures are available, or cross the street to the **Redlands Building,** where city information is also available.

Proceed downtown and head immediately for **Eilenberger's Bakery,** 512 North John Street, where you can start your tour with a cup of coffee and a luscious home-baked pastry (my idea of the way to start any bicycle tour). Famous for their apricot and nut cakes, which are shipped all over the world, Eilenberger's has been in business since 1898, and in its present location since 1918.

From there you may want to ride around the **Historic Downtown** area (a self-guided walking tour is offered by the convention and visitors bureau) or visit the two museums of note in town: the **Howard House Museum,** 1011 North Perry Street, (903) 584-3225 (open by appointment), or **The Museum for East Texas Culture,** 400 Micheaux Street, (903) 723-1914, open Tuesday through Sunday. The **Anderson County Courthouse and Old Town Square,** between Crawford Street and Lacy Street, exemplifies late 1880s' neoclassical architecture and features a double interior spiral staircase and a beautiful stained glass dome. The courthouse is open Monday through Friday, 8 A.M. to 5 P.M.

Park your car at Palestine State Park, which is located 6 miles east of the city on Highway 84. From the park entrance, go left on Highway 84 toward Palestine for 2.2 miles to the junction of Highway 84 and FM 323. Go left on FM 323. About 10 miles out, or just before the intersection of FM 323 and FM 1817, you'll find **Becky's Country Store** which is the last store for nearly 10 miles. Continue on FM 323 for 6 more miles to the junction with Highway 294 and take a left on Highway 294. Look for a couple of stores in **Denson Springs,** about 2.5 miles down Highway 294. After another 2.5 miles, you'll come to the junction with FM 228; turn right. After 2.9 miles, turn left on FM 3016. After 4.4 miles, turn left on FM 227, and enter the **Davy Crockett National Forest.** Continue 3 miles until FM 227 dead-ends into Highway 21. Turn left toward the small town of **Weches.**

Just before you get to Weches, you will see the turn into the **Tejas Mission State Historical Park.** A guide to new state parks in

Texas lists this one as an "overlooked treasure," and after pedaling through you'll see why. Secluded and tranquil amid the piney woods, it offers shady spots for picnicking or camping, and hiking trails if you want a break from your bike. It also houses a replica of the **Mission San Francisco de los Tejas,** the first East Texas mission, established by the Spanish in 1690 on the Neches River in response to LaSalle's French colony on the Texas coast. In addition, the **Rice Family Log Home,** an interesting example of the log home construction typical of the early Texas settlers, is open for exploration.

Because Tejas Mission Park is 35 miles from Palestine, it is a nice place to camp on your first night. If you don't have camping equipment, however, continue on to **Alto.**

Turn left out of the state park entrance and continue on Highway 21 toward Alto. Highway 21 is a more trafficked artery than those you've been on so far, but it's wide and flat enough for safe riding. The entrance to **Caddoan Mounds State Historical Park,** an important archeological site, lies 6 miles down Highway 21. Caddoan Mounds was a frontier settlement and ceremonial center of the early Caddos, the westernmost group of mound builders whose culture spanned from 1,000 B.C. to 1,500 A.D. Investigations at Caddoan Mounds have added tremendously to the understanding of prehistoric Indian culture in Texas. You can learn more about this culture through interpretive exhibits, an audio-visual program, and a 3/4-mile trail tour around the mounds, which includes a burial mound and a village area.

From Caddoan Mounds Park, continue eastward on Highway 21 to Alto. The town of Alto is 6 miles away, but the only overnight accommodation, **the Lincrest,** is 4 miles east of town on Highway 21. If you need to stock up on snacks or supplies for the next day, do it in Alto because there won't be another store until **Douglass,** which is 7 miles past the Lincrest.

DAY TWO: Alto to Nacogdoches

From Alto, continue east on Highway 21 to Douglass. Even though you've been on the road for only 7 miles, check your water and supplies in Douglass, because there's nothing else for the rest of the 20 or so miles into Nacogdoches. In Douglass, turn right onto FM 225. Five miles south of Douglass, FM 225 takes a sharp left turn. Continue on FM 225 about 4 miles to Lake Nacogdoches and an exhilarating downhill. On weekends, expect slightly more traffic on the stretch of FM 225 from the lake into town, but the traffic is still not a problem. Stay on FM 225 for about 8 more miles to the outskirts of Nacogdoches.

Spend the rest of day two exploring historic Nacogdoches. One of the oldest cities in Texas, Nacogdoches will remind you of a town out of the Antebellum South with its plantation-style homes, great magnolia trees, and fragrant hydrangea and wisteria vines. The city grew from the **Mission Nuestra Senora de Guadalupe,** established by the Spanish in 1716 alongside a village of the Nacogdoche Indians, and prospered as an outpost on the El Camino Real, a major route through Texas to San Antonio and beyond.

Again, a good place to start any exploration of Nacogdoches is at the **Chamber of Commerce,** on North Street (also Highway 59) across from the **Stephen F. Austin University** campus. From there, you'll be close to one of Texas' most historic buildings, the **Old Stone Fort,** between Griffith Street and Clark Street. Built in 1779, this old edifice has housed a trading post, a Spanish garrison and government headquarters, the first two newspapers in Texas, and an archival repository. It was even the site of the Battle of Nacogdoches in 1832 in which the Mexican Army, trying to quell the growing Texas rebellion, demanded that the citizens lay down their arms. The Mexican commander finally ended the skirmish by allowing the citizens to keep their arms if they promised not to use them against the Mexican troops. Predictably, their promise didn't last long. The rest, as they say, is history.

The **Adolphus Sterne Home and Hoya Museum,** which is located on Lanana Street, just a few blocks off Highway 21, displays East Texas memorabilia from the colonization to the postrevolution eras. Constructed by Adolphus Sterne in 1828, it stood as the center of social and political life in this area until the death of its second owner, Joseph vanderHoya, in 1897. In 1833, Sam Houston was baptized a Catholic here in accordance with the Mexican requirement that all landholders be Catholics. (Records at the Old Baptist Church in Independence show he was baptized there as well. He was either a true politician or covering all his bases!) Much of the home on display today is original.

Also on Lanana Street, a few blocks past the museum, is the **Oak Grove Cemetery,** where you will find the gravesites of Thomas J. Rusk, the first secretary of war of the Texas Republic, and three other signers of the Texas Declaration of Independence.

From the cemetery, take Price Street to Mound Street. Ride down Mound Street and gawk at the wonderful western Victorian homes. You might also want to ride through the Stephen F. Austin campus again toward **Millard's Crossing,** which is a little beyond the downtown area. It's a collection of early Texas homes and a museum resembling a small village. Tours are available Monday through Satur-

THE BACKWOODS OF EAST TEXAS

day, 9 A.M to 4 P.M. and Sunday 1:30 P.M. to 4:30 P.M. Call (409) 564-6631 for additional information.

DAY THREE: Nacogdoches to Rusk

From Nacogdoches, take Powers Street off North Street (Highway 59). It turns sharply to the right and becomes Old Tyler Road or FM 1638. In 2.5 miles, it crosses the Loop 224 (Highway 59) bypass. Continue on FM 1638 for another 2.1 miles to the junction with FM 343. Turn left on FM 343.

Continue on FM 343 for 12.6 miles across **Bayou Loco** and **Little Bayou Loco** into **Looneyville.** There's nothing but a gas station/convenience store in Looneyville, but you might want to stop because there isn't much for the remaining 21 miles or so into Rusk. From Looneyville, you continue on FM 343, which merges with FM 225 here. Turn left on FM 343/225 and go 1.2 miles where FM 343 veers off to the right. Take this right fork and continue on FM 343 into Rusk.

Continue on FM 343 through Rusk; it forms a loop around the city. Turn left on Highway 84 (it has a good shoulder) and continue just less than 2 miles to the entrance of the **Texas State Railroad Park and depot,** where you'll board the train for the return trip to Palestine. The Texas State Railroad allows bicycles in its baggage car, but you must notify them in advance. The Texas State Railroad runs Saturday and Sunday from March through May, and Thursday through Monday from

---

Route Options: There are a couple of options for shortening this ride. One way is to ride to Nacogdoches the first day, bypassing Mission Tejas and Caddoan Mounds State Parks. To do this, continue on FM 924 (do not turn on FM 228) to Alto. In Alto, take Highway 21 to Nacogdoches, making it a 61.5-mile first day; the mileage and route for the second day remain the same.

Another option is to make it a one-day ride by proceeding directly from Palestine to Alto to Rusk. But if you go this way, you'll miss Nacogdoches. This route is 40 miles long if you take the train back to Palestine; 65 miles if you ride. The best way from Alto to Rusk is to take Highway 69 just out of Alto and to turn right on FM 851. Go 4 miles to the junction of FM 241. Take a left and follow FM 241 into Rusk. The state park and train station are 3 miles west of Rusk on Highway 84.

May through mid-August. From mid-August to the end of October, it returns to its Saturday and Sunday schedule. Call (903) 683-2561 or 1-800-442-8951 (in Texas only) for further information on schedules, rates, and reservations.

ACCOMMODATIONS: Ash-Bowers Bed and Breakfast, 301 South Magnolia Street, Palestine, (903) 729-1935. **Best Western,** 1601 West Palestine Avenue, Palestine, (903) 723-4655. **The Ramada Inn,** 1101 East Palestine Avenue, Palestine, (903) 723-7300 or 1-800-657-1800. **Country Christmas Tree Farm or Sunday House Bed and Breakfast,** Route 3, Box 3566 (off of Highway 19 on County Road 465 in Bois D'Arc), Palestine, (903) 729-4836. **Days Inn,** 1100 East Palestine Avenue, Palestine, (903) 729-3151. **The Wiffletree Inn,** 1001 North Sycamore, Palestine, (903) 723-6793. **The Lincrest Lodge Guest Farm** (bed and breakfast), P.O. Box 799 (located 4 miles east of town on Highway 21), Alto, (409) 858-2223. **Best Western Nacogdoches Inn,** 2020 Stallings Drive Northwest (Loop 224/U.S. Highway 59), Nacogdoches, (409) 569-0880 or 1-800-528-1234. **Blueberry Hill Farm Inn** (bed and breakfast), Route 6, Box 1300 (8 miles north of Loop 224), Nacogdoches, (409) 564-7200. **Holiday Inn,** 3400 South Street, Nacogdoches, (409) 564-0261 or 1-800-465-4329. **Tol Barret House** (bed and breakfast), Route 4, Box 9400 (off of FM 2863, 3 miles south of town) Nacogdoches, (409) 569-1249.

CAMPING: Palestine State Park, Highway 84 (6 miles east of Palestine), Palestine, 75802, (214) 683-5126. **Triple-B Farms Campground,** Route 6 Box 2720 (12 miles north of Nacogdoches off of County Road 141), Nacogdoches, (409) 564-8919.

FOR MORE INFORMATION: Palestine Convention and Visitors Bureau, P.O. Box 1177, Palestine, Texas, 75802, (903) 723-3014 or (903) 729-6066. **Nacogdoches County Chamber of Commerce,** 1801 North Street, P.O. Drawer 63, Nacogdoches, Texas, 75963, (409) 564-7351.

Texas Independence Trail Tour

DAY ONE: Chappell Hill to Brenham

Ride through Washington County and you'll understand why the Texas pioneers chose to settle in the fertile Brazos River Valley. You'll pedal past miles of gently rolling pastureland (on the pavement some of the "rolls" won't seem so gentle!), flecked with graceful live oaks, wildflowers, and grazing livestock. Many of the "Old Three Hundred," the original families Stephen F. Austin brought to Texas, colonized this area and some of their homes—and graves—can be seen. Wealthy cotton planters from Louisiana, Alabama, and Mississippi, sensed new opportunities for the expansion of their empires and built plantation estates here. Several of Texas' oldest educational institutions were once located here, giving rise to the common reference to the region as "The Athens of Early Texas." Not surprisingly, Texas' roots as a republic and as a state are also in Washington County.

One of the loveliest times to ride through this area is during wildflower season, which runs roughly from the middle of March to the end of April, when native Texas wildflowers such as the bluebonnet, Indian paintbrush, winecup, daisy, and sunflower abound. Be forewarned, however, that Washington County is a prime place to view and photograph wildflowers, so vans full of rubberneckers may be as prolific

- **Starting point:** Chappell Hill (loop)
- **Route:** day one—Chappell Hill to Brenham
         day two—Brenham to Chappell Hill
- **Mileage:** day one—42.5 miles
         day two—30.5 miles
         total—73 miles
- **Terrain:** rolling to hilly
- **Best time to ride:** March and April, for wildflowers, and all fall
- **Traffic conditions:** light (except on Highway 105)
- **Road Conditions:** good

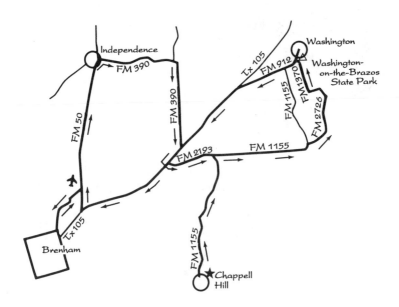

as the plant life. Make sure you are as visible as possible to motorists who may be watching the wildflowers more than the road. Wear bright colors, use a rearview mirror, and be aware.

This tour begins and ends in **Chappell Hill,** located on Highway 290 between Houston and Austin. There's no central parking lot, so park off Main Street and be extra careful not to block driveways. This quaint town, founded in 1849 by southern planters, deserves to be explored. A wonderful start would be with a stay or at least a tour at the **Browning Plantation,** a painstakingly restored cotton plantation home built in 1857 by Colonel W. W. Browning, a scion of early Chappell Hill. Now a bed and breakfast with a few twentieth-century touches, such as a patio and pool, this estate is located south of Highway 290 near the intersection of FM 1155 and FM 1371 (look for the small white signs). It's less than a half mile down a gravel road to the gate, but the trip is well worth the minor inconvenience. For a tour or reservations, call (409) 836-6144.

While you're still on the south side of Highway 290, ride by the **St. Stanislaus Catholic Church,** which grew from a mission established in 1889. The original building was destroyed in the great storm of 1900, the same one that nearly wiped Galveston off the map. The present building dates back to 1924.

The **Chappell Hill United Methodist Church,** organized in 1847, and the **Chappell Hill Historical Museum,** housed in a building of the old **Chappell Hill Female College,** are also worth a visit. Museum hours are Tuesday through Saturday 10 to 3, and Sunday 1 to 3, but you might want to call (409) 836-6033 to confirm. (I have visited a couple of times during these hours only to find the doors locked.) After your ride, stroll down Chappell Hill's Main Street and stop at the **S&B Drugstore** for some hand-dipped Blue Bell (the Texas-made ice cream locals swear by) or collapse at **Bever's Country Cooking,** located in an historic old home, for a full-blown meal complete with homemade dessert. Unfortunately, most of these places are closed on Sunday, but schedules do change, so check.

To begin your ride, proceed north on FM 1155, which is also Chappell Hill's Main Street. Continue for 7.5 miles on one of the prettiest stretches of ranch road anywhere. Because the prevailing wind will probably be at your back and this stretch is more downhill than uphill, you'll fly to the intersection of FM 1155 and FM 2193. It will appear that FM 1155 dead-ends, but it actually continues to the right. Turn right and continue on FM 1155 for 5.6 miles to FM 2726; turn right. Continue 3.3 miles to FM 1370 (there's a store at this intersection, but it's usually closed on Sundays), and turn left. Follow FM 1370 3.5 miles until it dead-ends into FM 912/1155.

Turn right on FM 912/1155 and go less than a mile to the entrance of **Washington-on-the-Brazos State Historical Park.** This picturesque park, which unfortunately is for day use only, features a replica of the hall in which the Texas Declaration of Independence was signed on March 2, 1836. The building is a faithful reproduction of the original, using designs and materials described in writings from the period, and archaeologists claim it is located on the same site. The **Star of the Republic Museum** is also in the park, along with the refurbished **home of Anson Jones,** who was the last president of the Texas Republic.

Not much is left of the once-thriving community of Washington, as it was known then. The town originally grew around **Robinson's Ferry,** an important crossing on the Brazos River. Washington prospered during the years of the Texas Republic (1836–45), claiming 400 citizens, a newspaper, boys' and girls' academies, and a number of general merchandise stores offering everything from "champagne wine" to spelling books. In 1842, Sam Houston persuaded the government of the Republic to relocate to Washington, and it was here in 1845 that the Texas Congress voted in favor of annexation to the United States. According to the annexation agreement, Texas could have been divided into as many as five states.

Because the park is 20 miles into your ride, it makes a nice picnic stop on the first day. There's a shaded picnic area on the banks of the Brazos, and a store just outside the park entrance that sells drinks and snacks. The park is open from 8 A.M. to sunset seven days a week; the Star of the Republic Museum is open daily from 10 A.M. to 5 P.M. from March through August, and Wednesday through Sunday, 1 to 5 P.M. from September through February.

To continue your ride, go left out of the park entrance on FM 912 (FM 1155). After 2 miles, FM 1155 cuts left, but you will continue straight on FM 912. Continue for 3 miles to Highway 105. Turn left (west) on Highway 105. Although this is a busy thoroughfare, there is a wide shoulder. Follow it for 5.6 miles to FM 2193, which will be on your left. There's also a store on your right, which is open weekdays and Sundays after 10 A.M.

Note: If you want to make this a day ride, turn left on FM 2193, then right on FM 1155 and take it back to Chappell Hill. This will be approximately 40 miles round-trip.

Continue on Highway 105 (do not turn left on FM 2193) to **Brenham,** which is the seat of Washington County. About a mile and a half after the junction with FM 2193, Highway 105 loses its shoulder and poses more challenging riding. You will only have to stay on this narrower section for 4.4 miles, however, before turning right onto FM 50. Continue on FM 50 for 1.2 miles to Airport Road and turn left. When this splits, follow the fork to the left where the road becomes Old Independence Road. Don't despair when this road turns to gravel. You aren't lost! The gravel, which is mostly hard-packed and only continues for .8 mile, isn't as bad as the traffic on Highway 105. Follow Old Independence Road past the **Washington County Fairgrounds** and a city recreational park to East Horton Street.

Take a right on East Horton Street (FM 577), which has a nice wide shoulder. Follow East Horton Street to North Park Street, go left, and follow the signs to **Historic Downtown Brenham.** Here you can stop at the **This Must Be Heaven** ice cream and sandwich shop for some more of that luscious Blue Bell, which incidentally is made in Brenham, or continue to the classic downtown cafe **The Fluff Top Roll Restaurant.** Also notable in the downtown area is **The Great Ant Street Restaurant,** which serves American country cuisine in a restored saloon and, you guessed it, more hand-dipped Blue Bell. But for a true Main Street America experience, check out the two places that are mainstays of southern small town squares: the **Perry's 5 & 10** and the **Western Auto.** After all, where *did* you get your first bicycle?

If it's not too late and you haven't overdosed on Blue Bell, you can ride to the **Blue Bell Creameries,** home of their self-proclaimed "best ice cream in the country." From downtown, go south on South Austin Street (Business Highway 36) to Tom Green Street and turn left. As you leave downtown on South Austin, watch for the ornate gingerbread house on your right. This Victorian is still a private residence open only during the Spring Fling and Heritage Homes Tour in March. When Tom Green Street hits South Horton Street (FM 577), turn left and the Blue Bell Creameries will be on your right in less than a mile.

Tours of Blue Bell Creameries are offered during the week but inexplicably not on weekends or holidays (when most tourists tour). However, the Visitor's Center and Gift Shop is open weekdays 8 A.M. to 5 P.M. and from 9 A.M. to 3 P.M. on Saturdays.

DAY TWO: Brenham to Chappell Hill

To leave Brenham, turn right on South Horton Street (FM 577) and go north (the street will become North Horton) to retrace your path on Old Independence Road to FM 50. Just to confuse you, the street sign names this "Old Prairie Road." Take it to the right nonetheless, past the fairgrounds and park again. Continue on it, taking the right fork this time onto Airport Road, which dead-ends into FM 50. Go left on FM 50 and proceed 7.3 miles to **Independence.**

There's probably more Texas history per square foot packed into this tiny hamlet than in any other town in the state. Named in 1836 in recognition of the recently signed Texas Declaration, Independence became home, headquarters, and gathering place for many heroes of the Texas Revolution and veterans of the Civil War. The **Coles home,** built in 1823, still remains, as does the **Toalson home,** now a private residence, the **Hoxey house** and the **Robertson home. Mrs. Sam Houston's home** also remains, and in fact, she is buried here. General Sam Houston was buried in Huntsville, but Margaret Moffette Lea, the general's widow, died in Independence of highly contagious yellow fever and her body was buried hastily to prevent the disease's spread.

Two branches of Baylor University (one for men and one for women) were established here, and the ghostly columns of one of the main buildings guard the hill in **Old Baylor Park,** just past Independence on FM 390 west. Baylor University's relocation to Waco in 1886 marked the beginning of Independence's decline.

At the intersection of FM 50 and FM 390, under a grove of gnarled live oaks, stands **Old Independence Baptist Church,** home of the first Baptist congregation in Texas. Next door is the **Texas Baptist**

Historical Center, a charming little museum with exhibits and the best place to obtain information on the area. The museum is open Wednesday through Saturday, from 10 A.M. to 4 P.M. and on Sunday from 1 P.M. to 5 P.M. (by reservation only). Call (409) 836-5117 for more information.

If you're lucky, you'll run into Independence Baptist Church's jovial minister, Reverend Paul Sevar. A wealth of information about early Independence, Reverend Sevar loves to tell anecdotes about Sam Houston, who was baptized here and who reportedly whittled during church services.

From Independence, turn east on FM 390. There's a store just off the road to the right not even one-quarter of a mile past the intersection of FM 50 and FM 390. Continue on FM 390 (La Bahia Road) for 4.3 miles, where it takes a sharp turn to the right. Follow it another 4.7 miles to Highway 105.

Turn right on Highway 105 and go a little more than a mile to FM 2193 and turn left. You'll enjoy a couple of steep roller coaster-type hills on this stretch (depending on your definition of enjoyment) until it meets FM 1155 2.5 miles later. Turn right on FM 1155 and retrace this road to Chappell Hill.

ACCOMMODATIONS: The Browning Plantation, Route 1 Box 8 (located ½ mile south of FM 1155 and Highway 290 intersection on Browning Lane), Chappell Hill, (409) 836-6144 or (713) 661-6761. **The Mulberry House,** P.O. Box 5, 2447 Chestnut Street (1 block off Main Street) Chappell Hill, (409) 830-1311. **Stagecoach Inn,** P.O. Box 339, Main Street at Chestnut Street, Chappell Hill, (409) 836-9515. **The Brenham House** (bed and breakfast), 705 Clinton Street, Brenham, (409) 830-0477. **Heartland Country Inn** (14-room bed and breakfast), Route 2, Box 446, at Palestine Road and County Road 68 (10 miles northeast of Brenham), Brenham, (409) 836-1864. **Hill Top Inn,** Highway 36 South, Brenham, (409) 836-7915. **Preference Inn,** Highway 290 (at Becker Drive), Brenham, (409) 830-1110. **Secrets** (bed and breakfast), 405 Pecan Street, Brenham, (409) 836-4117.

CAMPING: Artesian Park (RV park), Route 6 Box 6357, on Highway 290 West (7 miles west of Brenham), Brenham, (409)836-0680.

FOR MORE INFORMATION: Washington County Convention and Visitor Bureau, 314 South Austin, Brenham, Texas 77833, (409) 836-3695. (They also offer a more complete list of bed and breakfasts in the area.)

The Big Thicket Tours

The Big Thicket is less a place than a feeling—a feeling of lifestyles flash-frozen in time, of slower-paced existences, of isolation, and mystery. Yes, there are Wal-Marts and traffic, but there are also wonderful examples of Big Thicket heritage everywhere. Restaurants serve up embarrassing quantities of locally grown specialties, and fiddlers' duels and ghost story telling contests highlight local festivals. While I was researching the area for these tours, an election was held to decide whether to improve the road through a quiet little community anachronistically called **Hoop and Holler.** The proposition failed. One resident was quoted as saying, "Those who want to see us badly enough can get here on the road we have. The rest don't matter."

Technically, the Big Thicket is a heavily forested area occupying most of southeast Texas. It's frequently referred to as the "biological crossroads of North America" because it is the confluence of so many ecosystems: southeastern swamp, eastern forest, coastal plain, and southwestern desert. The **Big Thicket National Preserve** consists of 86,000 acres separated into 12 units, each showcasing a different ecotone, or meeting of habitats and plant populations.

Although the Alabama and Coushatta Indians hunted the Big Thicket, they lived on its periphery, and whites settled this area relatively late because the land was difficult to clear. During the Civil War, gangs of Union sympathizers loyal to Sam Houston, who opposed Texas' secession, hid out in the Big Thicket. They used the call of the jayhawk to communicate and identify each other in the forest, and hence were dubbed the "Jayhawkers." A Confederate colonel grew wise to this activity and, in what's referred to as "Kaiser's Burnout," set fire to a large area of the Big Thicket, flushing out many of the Jayhawkers.

Lumbering and oil exploration continued the development of the Big Thicket, but unfortunately they doomed the original woods. What was once a 3.5 million-acre forest now covers less than 300,000 acres, with 86,000 acres protected from further development by the National Preserve.

☐

The Steinhagen Lake Loop

This tour begins and ends at the **Woodville Inn** in the center of **Woodville.** Even if you don't stay here, begin your tour at the **Tyler County Chamber of Commerce**—a good source of additional maps and information on the area. The traffic will be heaviest around Woodville, but is otherwise very light.

Leave the Woodville Inn from the back, which is on Charlton Street. Across Dogwood Street from the inn (on the corner of Charlton and Dogwood) is the **Allan Shivers Library and Museum,** housed in a Victorian home. It contains memorabilia of Allan Shivers, governor of Texas from 1949 to 1957, who grew up in Woodville. It's open on weekdays from 9 A.M. to 5 P.M. and on Saturdays from 10:00 A.M. to 2:00 P.M. Call (409) 283-3709 for a guided tour.

From the front door of the museum, go left on Charlton across Bluff Street (the main street, and also Highway 190) to the **Courthouse Square,** where there are a number of historical markers and monuments. Across from the courthouse, is the **Wheat home,** built in 1848. There's an interesting historical marker in front, but the home is not open to the public. From the square, go west on Bluff Street. One and a half miles down Bluff Street (Highway 190) is **Heritage Village,** a museum and collection of historic buildings depicting life in the area from the 1840s to the 1900s.

On the Heritage Village site is the **Pickett House,** a boarding house-style, all-you-can-eat restaurant in an old school building. You may want to visit it after your ride so you can replenish your body with a generous helping of Big Thicket soul food. After paying the cashier in advance, help yourself to the beverage table, where cold buttermilk is one of the choices. The food is then wheeled up on a serving cart (there's too much to carry by hand). The day I visited the menu included

- **Starting point:** Woodville (loop)
- **Mileage:** 45 miles
- **Terrain:** gently rolling to flat
- **Best time to ride:** March and April
- **Traffic conditions:** light
- **Road conditions:** fair

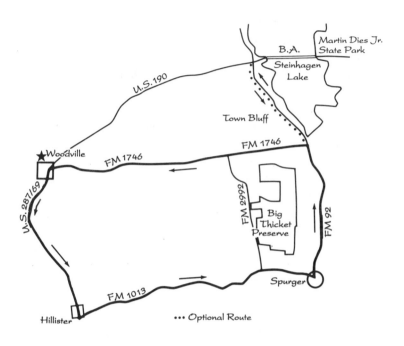

fried chicken and chicken and dumplings, turnip greens, candied yams, lima beans, cole slaw, biscuits, corn bread, and watermelon rind pickles on the side, with peach cobbler for dessert. A word of caution: this is unabashedly not '90s food, so granola-heads may want to steer clear of it.

While you're on Bluff Street, stop by the **Lazy J Peanut Ranch,** 305 West Bluff, which specializes in Texas-flavored roasted peanuts and peanut butter available for chomping on the spot or shipping around the country. Choose from flavors such as jalapeño, chili, or hickory smoked. Or try the mesquite-flavored peanut butter—you can order everything from a gift pack to a case. If you want to order some later, call 1-800-852-NUTS. (I am not making this up!)

To begin your ride, leave town on Beach Street which crosses Bluff Street (Highway 190) a mile east of Heritage Village. Go south on Beach Street, which will suddenly become "Beech" for no apparent reason. Follow it to Cobb Mill Road. If you turn right on Cobb Mill and go to the fifth building on the right, you can visit the **Texas Rocker Company,** where handcrafted single or two-seated rockers are made from hardwood ash. To continue on your route turn right and get back on Cobb Mill, proceeding west until it hits Highway 287/69. Turn right.

The traffic on this stretch may seem unnerving at first, but there is a shoulder, and the traffic thins out dramatically after only a couple of miles. Continue on Highway 287/69 for 7 miles to **Hillister.** Here you'll find **The Homestead Restaurant,** which serves steaks, seafood, chicken, and mouth-watering desserts, but is open for lunch only on Sunday (it's open from 5 to 10 Thursday through Saturday). Call (409) 283-7324 to confirm their hours.

Turn left on FM 1013 in Hillister, but take a minute to check your supplies because it's 13 miles to **Spurger** and there's nothing in between. After 10 miles, you'll come to the junction with FM 2992. If you want to hike the **Beech Woods Trail** through the Big Thicket Preserve, turn left here and go 2 miles. Otherwise, continue to Spurger and turn left on Highway 92.

In 7 miles you'll come to the cluster of establishments known as **Town Bluff.** There's a store here and a picnic area with a scenic overlook from where you can see the **Neches River** and the **Town Bluff Dam,** which creates **B. A. Steinhagen Lake** (also known by locals as **Dam B**). This was once a major port on the Neches River connecting the area with the Gulf of Mexico, but the construction of the railroad nearby caused its decline. If you'd like to see more of the lake and picnic at one of the parks on its shores, continue on Highway 92 for 5 miles to the intersection with Highway 190. The day-use section of **Martin Dies State Park** is off Highway 190 just a couple of miles down.

If you choose this detour, however, I would not recommend returning to Woodville on Highway 190, or even riding across the lake on 190, for that matter. It's a major east-west thoroughfare with a rough shoulder that comes and goes. Retrace the 5 miles to Town Bluff. Whether you take the detour, from Town Bluff, go west on FM 1746 and ride the 14 miles back to Woodville.

ACCOMMODATIONS: The Woodville Inn, 201 North Magnolia Street (at Highway 190 and Highway 287/69), Woodville, (409) 283-3741. **The Getaway Guest House Bed and Breakfast,** located 2 miles off of FM 1013 out of Hillister at the end of Pope Mill Lane (on Theuvenn Creek on the edge of the Big Thicket), Hillister, (409) 283-7244.

CAMPING: Jones Country (formerly country singer George Jones' estate), Route 1 Box 265, on Highway 255 (7 miles north of Woodville), Colmesneil, (409) 837-5463.

FOR MORE INFORMATION: Tyler County Chamber of Commerce, 507 North Pine Street, Woodville, Texas 75979, (409) 283-2632.

The Big Sandy Creek Tour

Begin your tour of this area with a visit to the **Alabama-Coushatta Indian Reservation,** on Highway 190, 16 miles east of Livingston. These two tribes have lived in the Big Thicket area for more than 150 years and were always friendly to the white settlers colonizing the area. Some helped Sam Houston in the Texas Revolution and others served in the Confederate Army during the Civil War. Sam Houston succeeded in securing a reservation for them during the 1850s, but it wasn't until the 1930s that the United States government followed through in completing the reservation. About 500 members of the United Tribes now live and work on the reservation grounds, which include a museum, Indian village, craft and gift shop, and restaurant. Every night during the summer, and on weekends in the spring and fall, tribal dances are performed in the outdoor arena. Call (409) 563-4391 or 1-800-392-4794 for schedules and information.

You also may camp on the shores of **Lake Tombigbee.**

If you camp at the reservation, it will seem like a logical place to park your car and start your tour. However, it would add about 17 miles, including a nerve-wracking 4.5-mile stretch on Highway 190, which has no shoulder at this point, to your ride. I recommend parking your car at the trailhead for the **Big Thicket Woodlands Trail,** which is just off FM 1276. This takes you well off Highway 190, and the traffic is virtually nonexistent for most of the rest of this ride.

From Highway 190, go south on FM 1276 (it only goes one direction off 190). There will be a store at this intersection. Continue for 4 miles and watch for the Woodlands trailhead on the left. Park your car here.

- **Starting point:** Big Thicket Woodlands trailhead (loop; trailhead is off of Highway 190 outside of Livingston)
- **Mileage:** 60 miles
- **Terrain:** flat
- **Best time to ride:** March through June and September through December
- **Traffic conditions:** very light
- **Road conditions:** good

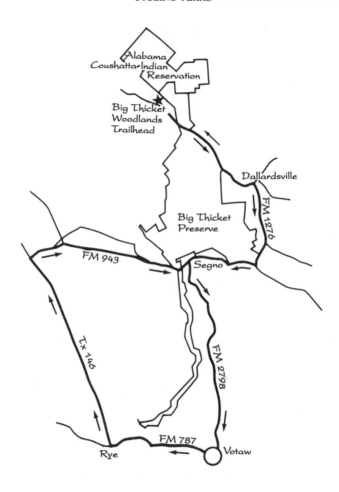

Continue on FM 1276 for 5 miles to **Dallardsville.** This is an exceptionally pretty road, twisting through vintage Big Thicket land-scapes. You'll pass in and out of the **Big Sandy Creek** portion of the Big Thicket Preserve. Because logging is prohibited in the preserve but allowed outside its boundaries, the area sometimes has an unfortunate mohawk-haircut look to it. However, there's plenty of lush vegetation left: virgin pine, magnolia, oak, and hickory blend with the rusty-colored soil found in this part of the thicket.

In Dallardsville you'll find a store or two, but not much else. Continue on FM 1276 to the intersection of FM 943, 4.3 miles further. Turn right on FM 943 and continue 3.8 miles to **Segno.**

In Segno, there's also a store, and the turn-off to FM 2798. Turn left and follow FM 2798 10 miles to **Votaw.** Votaw is only about 7 miles from the **Old Bragg Ghost Road**—a place full of local legend and lore. A rail spur once ran between here and what is now the ghost town

of **Bragg,** named for the Confederate General Braxton Bragg who settled here after the war. Legend holds that a brakeman was decapitated
in a train accident on this line and that he now wanders this lonely
8-mile stretch with a railroad lantern, searching for his head. Those
traveling the deserted road report having seen an eerie light that blinks
on and off. Many shrug it off, but no one has a logical explanation. The
road, which connects FM 1293 and FM 787 between Votaw and **Sara-
toga,** is soft sand and gravel and completely unmarked—after all, it is a
ghost road so you have to be psychic to figure out exactly where it is.

But if you have thick tires and even thicker skin and are into
out-of-body experiences, ride this road at dusk and see if you encounter
the Bragg Ghost. If you see the ghost, or if you even *think* you do, write
KKAS radio in **Silsbee** and tell them about your experience and they'll
send you a special certificate.

From Votaw, turn right on FM 787 toward **Rye,** 6 miles away. If
you're into this ghost thing now and enjoy deserted roads, turn right
about 4 miles down FM 787 toward Hoop and Holler. The road is unmarked, but there is a cluster of signs at its entrance. Unfortunately, the
road becomes gravel so you'll only be able to ride out and back. But for
3 miles or so it's pure cycling bliss. The road crosses **Menard Creek** on
a wooden plank bridge, and trees arch over, intertwining so thickly that
you'll think you're in the Black Forest.

When you return to FM 787, turn right and continue on to
Rye. In Rye, turn right on FM 146 (there's a store at this intersection)
and follow it 10 miles to FM 943. Turn right here and return to Segno.
From Segno, continue on FM 943 to FM 1276 and turn left. From here,
you'll retrace your route through Dallardsville to the Big Thicket Woodlands trailhead where you began.

ACCOMMODATIONS: Park Inn, 2500 Highway 59 South, Livingston, (409) 327-2525.

CAMPING: Lake Livingston State Park, on FM 3126 (7 miles out of
Livingston), (409) 365-2201. **Alabama-Coushatta Indian Reserva-
tion,** Route 3 Box 640, on Highway 190 (6 miles east of Livingston),
Livingston, (409) 563-4391 or 1-800-392-4794.

FOR MORE INFORMATION: Livingston Chamber of Commerce,
516 West Church, Livingston, Texas, 77351, (409) 327-4929.

THE HILL
COUNTRY
• • •
Lawrence Walker

It is often difficult to convince people who don't live in Texas—and even sometimes to convince those who do—that the state is not flat. It's a tough preconceived notion to set straight. Some people can't believe there are real, genuine hills in Texas even after they discover that a whole region of the state is commonly called the Hill Country. Texas is wide open, but it's not flat. Most of the state east of the Permian basin and the Caprock escarpment, which forms the sudden edge of the Great Plains, could be called rolling or gently rolling. But the Hill Country has got REAL HILLS.

The Texas Hill Country is a distinct geologic region with its own characteristic landforms, minerals, plants, and animals. It's not like anyplace else in the state, or for that matter, in the United States. On most maps, the Hill Country is called the Edwards Plateau, formed by the ancient (and currently inactive) Balcones Fault. The Balcones Fault runs just west of I–35 from about Georgetown southwest to San Antonio and about 10 to 15 miles north of U.S. 90 from San Antonio west to near Del Rio. The clearly visible Balcones Escarpment forms the eastern and southern boundaries of the Hill Country, a true edge where the Hill Country abruptly ends. (*Balcones* is Spanish for balcony, an appropriate name since the escarpment causes the land to jump up about 800 feet in elevation, from about 500 feet above sea level to well over 1000 feet.) East of the escarpment lies the pastoral gulf coastal prairie. To the south is the sun-bleached, mesquite-infested Brush Country. The northern and western boundaries of the Hill Country are not so clear cut, as they blend in with the motley Llano Estacado, but they roughly follow U.S. 190 from Belton west to Eldorado and U.S. 277 south from Eldorado to Del Rio.

What makes the Hill Country unique? It's the region's limestone and granite hills, covered by evergreen cedars (a kind of juniper) and oak trees—live oak, scrub oak, post oak, and a lively mix of other squatty hardwoods, including a few "lost" maples and pines. It's the many springs and clear, rushing streams and rivers, which are fed by the Edwards Aquifer. It's the limestone caverns, some formed by ancient earthquakes along the fault zone, others formed by the waters of receding oceans and underground waterways, and the curious outcroppings of granite along the Llano Uplift. And it's also the towering cypress trees that line its creekbeds and riverbanks, setting their paths apart from the surrounding terrain.

Hundreds of years ago, the Hill Country was home to bears, wolves, and mountain lions. But even now, the springs and rivers provide important habitat for some rare, specialized, and thus endangered species, such as the San Marcos Salamander and the Comal Blind Salamander. The thick cedars and oaks provide shelter and forage for a wide variety of distinctive songbirds, including the famous Black-capped Vireo and the Golden-cheeked Warbler. The caves, too, have their special wildlife— notably one of the largest bug-consuming bat populations in the world, which is mostly made up of the handy and admirable Mexican Freetail Bat. The Hill Country is, of course, famous for its more visible animals—armadillos (which, by the way, have only been in the area since about 1920), sheep, goats and, to many hunters' delight, white tail deer. (Wear loud colors when you ride in late fall!)

Considering that the Hill Country spreads west from the steps of the state capitol in Austin, the region remained surprisingly isolated until the 1940s when a young United States congressman named Lyndon Johnson fought to get electric power and some paved roads for his home turf. Johnson was instrumental in getting a series of sizable dams built along the Colorado River (the Texas Colorado, not the Colorado River that runs through Colorado, Utah, and Arizona). The resulting Highland Lakes, set against the photogenic relief of the surrounding hills, are considered the loveliest large lakes in the state. And now thanks to the German pioneers, LBJ, Lady Bird Johnson (who took it upon herself to create a beautify-the-highways campaign), and the good graces of the Texas Highway Department, the Hill Country is, in its own semiwild and scrubby kind of way, perhaps the most consistently handsome and tastefully preserved region of Texas.

Cyclists like hills. Or I should say, cyclists learn to like hills, to love them, and even to crave them. (If you don't think you like them now, after a few days, or maybe after a week or two, you will gradually get your climbing legs.) Hills make for good scenery, and they provide both challenge and exhilaration; they give cyclists a chance to display (at least to themselves) their newfound or enduring strength and to perfect their craft, style, and *bravery* (which Hemingway defined as "grace under pressure"). As you will certainly find out, descriptions of hills are subjective. Their frequency, their size, their difficulty and their connection with the meaning of life are relative. One rider's hill is another's rolling terrain, and yet another's gently rolling terrain. Some flatland-bound Texans think a big hill is a mountain, but the Texas hills are not mountains; you've got to go west of the Pecos for those. Most of the individual climbs in the Hill Country are 100 to 1,000 feet long and gain 100 to 200 feet. There are very few climbs that last more than a mile or two or that rise more than 400 feet without relief. On some roads, the hills come in rapid succession—roller coasters. On others, the ups and downs are isolated with broad valleys and flat (another relative term) stretches in between. You'll have to experience a variety yourself so you can come up with your own personal definition of a big hill, little hill, long hill, and short hill.

The Texas Hill Country has some advantages that even other hilly areas lack. Some of its towns are especially charming. Great country cafés, historic inns, and bed and breakfasts take a special liking to the Hill Country. Its townspeople seem especially hospitable. Its hidden county backroads offer seclusion with scenery, and its state of the art network of Farm-to-Market roads (FMs) are all beautifully designed and paved. The region's low-water crossings are not quite like those anyplace else. They are rather happy-go-lucky creatures, so close to and sometimes just under the surface of the water. When I was a kid, as we approached a crossing that had maybe five or six inches of water, I used to say we were "going swimming in the car." Well, even today in some places, if the water is flowing over the road, you can go swimming on your bicycle, but to avoid literally swimming with your bicycle, it's better to walk across because the wet crossings can be slick with moss or algae. And when things look serious, check that flood gauge! Still, low-water crossings, when it's sunny and the cypress tree leaves are a canopy of bright lime-colored needles (and there aren't any flash flood warnings), are some of the Hill Country's great delights. Another Hill Country advantage: the resident motorists are generally polite and cautious and, though there is that occasional exception, are usually patient as you grind it out up a hill. At least they hesitate instead of accelerating.

Finally, the Hill Country's weather is favorable. It is possible for the cycling season to last from mid-March to mid-November without temperatures ever dropping into the 30s. In the summer, the hills provide some relief. Temperatures tend to be 5 to 10 degrees cooler in the Hill Country than in most of the rest of the state, especially in the river valleys and at night—which makes for good camping weather.

With a population of about 18,000, Kerrville is the largest town in the Hill Country. Most of the smaller burgs range from a few dozen to a few thousand. The land is still predominantly ranch country, so it can be a long way—say 30 miles or so—between people and even farther between services. The advantage to this is that, as long as you stay off the U.S. highways 290, 281, 183, and 90 and away from the lakes and favorite tubing spots on summer weekends, traffic will be light. A few Texas state highways, such as highways 46, 16, 71, and 29, can also have a bit too much traffic for comfort at times, as will several Ranch Roads, including RR 12 from San Marcos to Wimberley and RR 1431 from Cedar Park to Lago Vista. But once you get away from the cities and the fast lane, I'm sure you'll find many Hill Country roads to be just about cycling-perfect. On a good day out in the western reaches of the Hill Country, you might ride 10 to 15 miles without being passed by a single car.

On a more preparatory note, Kerrville is also the only town in the middle of the Hill Country with a bike shop. Fortunately, Kerrville is fairly close to a lot of the good riding in the region. There are other bike shops on the edge of the Hill Country in Round Rock, Austin, San Marcos, San Antonio, and Del Rio. Be prepared.

In this Hill Country section, I have created four very nice one-day loop rides for you, all of which have several options so you can choose the distance you want. The fourth loop ride is not exactly in the Hill Country as I have defined its boundaries—it's east of the Balcones Fault by about 30 miles—but it is hilly and a favorite with cyclists who usually consider it a Hill Country ride. The last tour is a wonderful four-day loop ride that begins and ends in Kerrville, taking you to some Hill Country classics: Medina, Bandera, Tarpley, Utopia, Garner State Park, Leakey, Vanderpool, Lost Maples State Natural Area, and Hunt as well as through four separate river valleys—the Medina, the Sabinal, the Frio and the Guadalupe. If I had only four days of my life to spend in the Hill Country, this is the tour I would take.

The Lost Pines Ride

This loop is one-third hills and two-thirds flat, making it a good introduction to riding hills, though that last third is pretty intense. The ride begins in **Bastrop,** one of Texas' oldest towns, steeped in the state's colonial history, and covers a nice section of **Colorado River** bottomland. After a break in Depression-era **Smithville,** Park Road 1 makes for a great climax with its lost pines and short, steep hills.

Begin at the **Bastrop County Courthouse.** Go north one block to Chestnut Street (Loop 150), and turn left (west). Pass through downtown Bastrop, cross the Colorado River on the old steel girder bridge, and take the first right after the bridge, which is unmarked here but is known as Old Austin Highway. In a mile, turn right on TX 71, and then left on TX 304 toward **Gonzales.** In 7.3 miles, veer left onto FM 2571 to Smithville. In 9.8 miles, you will reach TX 95 and Smithville. Turn left on TX 95. Explore Smithville (downtown and other stores are on Loop 230). Return to TX 95 and continue north, crossing the Colorado again, to TX 71. Follow the signs to **Buescher State Park** on FM 153. Turn left into **Buescher State Park,** and check in at the ranger station. Follow Park Road 1C 11 miles to Park Road 1A and **Bastrop State Park.** Exit Bastrop State Park onto Loop 150, and head west to Pine Street and the Bastrop courthouse.

- **Starting point:** Bastrop (loop)
- **Mileage:** 36 miles
- **Terrain:** Easy, rolling terrain except for 14 miles of short, steep hills on Park Road 1.
- **Best time to ride:** April is best for wildflowers, but good year-round when weather allows.
- **Traffic conditions:** Fairly light, very light, and kept to slow speeds on Park Road 1.
- **Road conditions:** Park Road 1 is narrow with no center stripe, but otherwise very good throughout the ride.

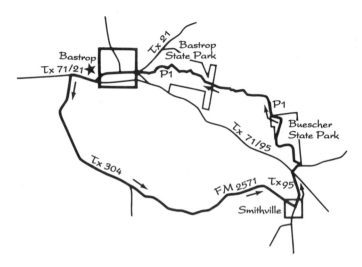

As mentioned before, Bastrop is not really in the Hill Country proper. The town is 30 miles east of the Balcones Fault, and is much different culturally and ethnically from the other towns in this section, all of which lie west of the fault. Park Road 1 runs 14 miles between the west entrance of Bastrop State Park and the east entrance of Buescher State Park. These parks are the bookends for a small area known as the **Lost Pines.** The area's loblolly pines are "lost" because they stand detached from the Texas pine forests by 100 miles. Texas cyclists often think of Park Road 1 as part of the Hill Country because it is hilly, yet these hills are detached from the Hill Country by 35 miles. Not only are the pines lost, so are the hills!

Bastrop is one of the oldest towns in Texas, and if you wander the side streets, you'll see many buildings dating from the mid- to late nineteenth century. Bastrop has the oldest weekly newspaper (established in 1853) and had the oldest drugstore in the state (until it burned a few years ago). The **Lock Drug Store** (pretty old itself—1905), at 1003 Main Street, is especially worth a visit because you can still get old-fashioned desserts at the marble soda fountain. The **Bastrop County Historical Museum** and the handsome **Old Bastrop County Jail** are worth exploring. If you'd like a brochure listing other buildings on the National Register of Historic Places, stop by the nearby visitors' kiosk.

As you leave downtown, you'll cross a steel girder bridge the likes of which you don't see too often anymore (though there is another nice one over the Colorado River in La Grange). Do be careful as you cross busy TX 71. The first 20 miles of this ride makes a broad swing around the south side of the Colorado River, closely following its meandering course. These are rich bottomlands unlike anything else you'll see on the other rides in this chapter. It was these fertile fields along the Colorado that attracted the early American colonists to Mexican Texas in the 1820s and 1830s. The big trees you see are mostly pecans, the state tree of Texas. A particularly nice stretch of the ride follows the elevated abandoned Missouri-Kansas-Texas (MKT or KATV) railroad tracks that parallel FM 2571.

One of the best reasons for taking this ride on a Saturday is so you can stop in Smithville for that favorite biker food—barbecue! Biker food or not, this is barbecue country. Both **Fuzzy's Bar B Que,** 110 Main, and **Zimmerhanzel's Bar B Que,** Loop 230 at the Colorado River bridge, are open Saturday and closed Sunday. They're great places to sample local flavors and local color. While you digest, visit the **Smithville Railroad Museum** at the foot of Main Street.

Now it's time for Park Road 1. You'll get settled into riding again as you head north on TX 95, cross under TX 71 and follow the signs to Buescher State Park and the eastern terminus of Park Road 1. The 1,730-acre park was set aside by the citizens of Smithville between 1933 and 1936. The Buescher Park entrance station is the last place for water and restrooms until Bastrop.

The hills along Park Road 1 are not like the hills in the true Hill Country. They are short and steep and covered with red dirt and pine needles, not limestone and cedars. The main reason these hills are so steep is that this special road was designed according to different engineering standards than regular state highways. There are no road cuts, and because the speed limit in the park is 25 miles per hour, the turns can be tight. It often seems as if this road winds around not to avoid steep grades but to intentionally attack the little hills straight on. This makes for one of the greatest cycling roads in the state. Car drivers usually expect there to be cyclists on the road. And the lost pines themselves are not cut back in a wide swath as they are on public highways; they come right to the edge of the road. So much of the park road is shaded—even at midday—when no other roads in the area are. Many cyclists make the pilgrimage from Houston and San Antonio and elsewhere just to ride these wonderful, almost private 14 miles back and forth.

On the western edge of Buescher State Park, you'll see the entrance to the University of Texas Cancer Center Science Park tucked away. This is a research facility for studies of potential cancer-causing substances found in the environment. The park also has a small lake and screened shelters.

Bastrop State Park, at the western end of the road, has a small lake and a swimming pool in case it's a hot summer's day, and a classy little golf course. The park also has a dozen cabins available. The citizens of Bastrop reserved this 3,500 acres of piney woods as parkland in 1938. From the Bastrop entrance station, it's a quick 2-mile descent back into town for a banana split at the Lock Drug Store.

ACCOMMODATIONS: Pine Point Inn, Texas Highway 71 East at Loop 150, Bastrop, (512) 321-1157. **The Pfeiffer House,** 1802 Main, Bastrop, (512) 321-2100.

CAMPING: Bastrop State Park, off of Highway 95/71 north of Smithville (see tour description for directions), (512) 321-2101. **Buescher State Park** off of FM 153 (see tour description for directions), (512) 237-2241.

FOR MORE INFORMATION: Bastrop Chamber of Commerce, 1009 Main Street, P.O. Box 681, Bastrop, Texas, 78602, (512) 321-2419.

LOCAL BIKE SHOP: Closest shops are in Austin, 32 miles west.

· ·

New Braunfels Day Ride

This great ride has a lot of attractions: Texas' largest cave open to the public, lake views, a magnificent run along the popular River Road and the fun historic district of **Gruene** (the German spelling for green, pronounced the same) at the end, which is great for taking a cool dip in the river, eating a good lunch and snapping up a souvenir T-shirt. **New Braunfels** itself is an interesting town with German heritage and German food, plus the watery attractions of **Landa Park, Camp Warnecke** and the **Schlitterbahn** (German for "water road"). This ride can be a peaceful delight in spring and fall, but if you want a ride with a bunch of frisky, frenetic wet-and-wild action, brave it in the summer. Be sure to take a bike lock if you think there is a chance you might want to tour the **Natural Bridge Caverns** or to take a dip in the **Guadalupe River.**

Begin at the gazebo in the middle of the square in New Braunfels, in front of the **Comal County Courthouse,** at the intersection of TX 46 (BUS TX 46) and San Antonio Street. (You can also start at Gruene.) Head south on South San Antonio Street. At the Conoco Sta-

- **Starting point:** New Braunfels (loop)
- **Mileage:** 66 miles
- **Terrain:** Slightly rolling from Gruene to Garden Ridge, then very hilly to River Road.
- **Best time to ride:** Do not attempt this ride on summer weekends! The hordes of tubers and partyers around Gruene and the River Road are terrible. Save this ride for weekends in spring and fall and weekdays in June.
- **Traffic conditions:** Heavy traffic in New Braunfels, moderate traffic south of New Braunfels to Garden Ridge and Natural Bridge Caverns, light traffic for the remainder of the ride (except as noted above).
- **Road conditions:** Pavement quality and lane width varies from state to county roads, but problem spots are rare.

---

tion, about ten blocks down San Antonio Street, veer right to continue another mile on Old San Antonio Street. Turn left onto Loop 337 to the I-35 frontage road. Turn right on the frontage road and immediately right again on FM 482. Just beyond the yellow blinking light at Solms Road, veer right to continue following FM 482. Two-tenths of a mile after Burke Road, turn right on Old Nacogdoches Road (watch for the little sign). When Old Nacogdoches Road ends 3 miles later, continue south on FM 2252. Two miles later, turn right on FM 3009 West to Natural Bridge Caverns Road. After visiting the caverns, continue north on FM 3009 to FM 1863. Turn left on FM 1863. After 7 miles, turn right on Upper Smithson Valley Road. Six miles later, at the junction with TX 46, continue straight on FM 3159 6.5 miles to **Startzville.** Turn right on FM 2673 to **Sattler,** another 6 miles. At Sattler, turn right on River Road. After 12 miles, turn left at the T intersection toward New Braunfels. After crossing TX 46, turn left on Rock Street to Gruene Road and Gruene. Continue on Gruene Road 1 mile to Common Street. When Common Street ends 1 mile after crossing TX 46 again, turn left on Union Street and go one block to North San Antonio Street. Turn right on North San Antonio Street and return to the courthouse square.

New Braunfels is a wonderful town and a great place to begin

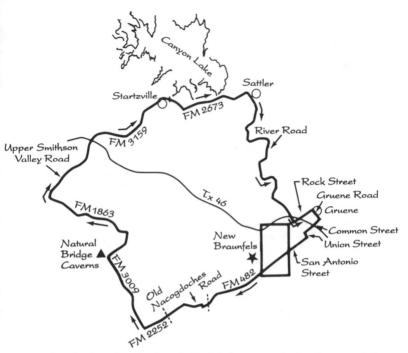

and end a bicycle ride. Landa Park is home to the headwaters of the world's shortest river (according to *Ripley's Believe It or Not*), the 3.5-mile long Comal, and one of the world's largest spring-fed pools. Camp Warnecke, a classic tubing resort, is just downriver, and then there is the phantasmagorical Schlitterbahn, billed as a "water theme park." New Braunfels displays its Germanic and nineteenth-century frontier roots at four museums: **the Sophienburg,** the **Lindheimer, Conservation Plaza,** and the **Museum of Texas Handmade Furniture.** Don't pass up the authentic German cuisine and a famous Old World bakery, **Naeglin's,** near the square.

Leaving the square, look for the venerable **Henne Hardware Company,** the state's oldest hardware store, and the stylish **Brauntex Theater.** As you ride the dozen miles south to **Garden Ridge,** you'll be following pieces of the old Austin-San Antonio road. You won't really be in the Hill Country but actually right on its edge. As you approach Garden Ridge, you'll be able to see signs of the **Balcones Escarpment** from the road. The land will rise up to your right and slope down to your left. There will be fields and scattered mesquite trees to the left, thick stands of oak and cedar to the right. These land form and flora differences denote the boundary of two distinct regions—the Gulf Coastal Prairie and the Hill Country.

The store at Garden Ridge makes a good stopping place to

load up on liquids and snacks before heading west into the hills. You'll climb from 640 feet up to 1400 feet, overlooking Canyon Lake. Billboards point the way to Natural Bridge Caverns, Texas' largest cave open to the public and one of its more lively and interesting as well. Four college students discovered the caverns in 1960, crawling through a tiny opening under the natural bridge you see at the modern entrance. The caverns have been forming for 140 million years, and the process continues, albeit one drip at a time. Natural Bridge is not known for its resident bat population, but a cave just a few miles away certainly is. **Bracken Cave,** recently protected, hosts the largest bat population in the world—over 2 million of these sophisticated and necessary mammals migrate to the cave each year.

Be sure to stock up on water and snacks at the cave; there aren't any stores for the next 20 miles. FM 1863 West has two quick crossings of Cibolo Creek underneath a striking cliff. Watch for the little yellow signs for Upper Smithson Valley Road, a quiet country lane that leads to **Smithson.** FM 3159 takes you up to the highpoint of today's ride, **Startz Hill,** elevation 1400 feet. From the road and a picnic area atop the climb you can see Canyon Lake hundreds of feet below. There is a sweeping downhill from Startz Hill to Startzville. Look for a few stores along FM 2673 in Startzville. There is another nice downhill into Sattler, where there are also several stores and a couple of cafés. Sattler used to be where Canyon Lake is now, but the town picked up and moved downstream when Canyon Dam was built.

The River Road from Sattler to the outskirts of New Braunfels is like no other road in the Hill Country. It is a narrow, winding county road that crosses the river several times, and it is lined with vacation getaways and ramshackle tubing (also known as "toobing") businesses. The Guadalupe along this stretch is lushly verdant and runs beneath towering limestone cliffs. Though not as manicured as Park Road 1, the River Road gives some of the same intimate feel of nature closing in on the edges of the road—unless you cruise this stretch at the height of summer, when the throngs of crazed, six-pack-toting "toobers" pack the roads and the river.

After four river crossings, the road swings up a good hill to a T intersection where you turn left toward New Braunfels. Just after crossing TX 46 at a stoplight, look for your left turn on Rock Street. This will take you to Gruene Road and another action-packed crossing of the Guadalupe. Gruene, Texas, sits on top of the high bank just beyond this crossing. **Gruene Hall** is said to be the oldest dancehall in Texas, and the rest of tiny Gruene has been set aside as a historic district. There are a few entertaining antique and craft stores, a winery, T-shirt shop, bed and breakfast, and, best of all, **The Grist Mill Restaurant.** This popular eating establishment is a converted old mill with seating in the cavernous interior or outside along a shady patio overlooking the Guadalupe 50 feet below. A stroll about Gruene and a lazy lunch at The Grist Mill are the perfect way to end your tour de Comal County.

From Gruene, continue east on Gruene Road to Commons Street. Take Commons south across the Guadalupe one last time and follow the route on city streets across the Comal River near the water flumes and the Schlitterbahn to the gazebo in the middle of the courthouse square. Two restaurants in New Braunfels that you might check out are: **Bavarian Village,** 212 West Austin Street, (512) 625-0815; **Krause's Café,** 148 South Castell Street, one block behind the **Faust Hotel,** (512) 625-7581.

ACCOMMODATIONS: Many motels are available along I-35 in New Braunfels; call the Chamber of Commerce for listings. **The Faust Hotel** (I recommend staying here), 240 South Seguin Street (BUS TX 46), New Braunfels, (210) 625-7791. **Gruene Mansion Inn** (bed and breakfast), 1275 Gruene Road, Gruene, (210) 629-2641.

CAMPING: Landa Trailer Park & Campground, 565 North Market Street, New Braunfels (210) 625-1211 (no state or public campgrounds nearby).

FOR MORE INFORMATION: Greater New Braunfels Chamber of Commerce, 390 South Seguin Street (BUS TX 46 East), New Braunfels, Texas, 78130 (210) 625-2385.

LOCAL BIKE SHOP: Closest shop is **B & J Bikeshop** at 8800 Broadway 25 miles south in San Antonio, (210) 826-0177.

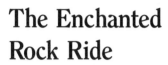

The Enchanted Rock Ride

This ride starts and ends in the Hill Country's handsomest and most touristy town, **Fredericksburg.** But it quickly takes you into the seemingly remote ranch lands of northern Gillespie County and the southern reaches of the **Llano Uplift** to two of Texas' Hill Country treasures—the **Willow City Loop** and **Enchanted Rock State Park.** This ride is not too difficult, and the rewards are great—especially if you can manage to ride this loop on a weekday when the bluebonnets are in bloom.

Start at the Gillespie County Courthouse, just west of U.S. 290 and TX 16 South. (You can also start at Enchanted Rock State Park.) Ride east about a mile to RR 1631. Turn left on RR 1631. Fourteen miles from this intersection (7 miles after FM 2721 veers off to the right), turn left on Herber Schaeffer Road (may be unmarked, but it's the only paved county road around). Turn left on RR 1323 to **Willow City.** The Willow City Loop is a local road that goes north from a sharp western bend of RR 1323. Follow the loop road 13 miles to TX 16. Turn left (south) on TX 16 and ride about 6 miles to Eckert Road, which will be on the right just before RR 1323 meets TX 16 on the left. You'll see a sign for **Rabke's Table Ready Meats;** go right (west) on Eckert Road. A mile beyond Rabke's and after crossing of **Crabapple Creek,** turn right on Crabapple Road, and follow it another 3 miles to RR 965. Turn right on RR 965 and take it to Enchanted Rock State Natural Area. After

- **Starting point:** Fredericksburg (loop)
- **Mileage:** 70 miles
- **Terrain:** moderate hills throughout ride
- **Best time to ride:** mid-March through June and September through late November
- **Traffic conditions:** Very light except approaching Enchanted Rock on weekends.
- **Road conditions:** Standard RR and FM roads. The Willow City Loop is narrow but paved.

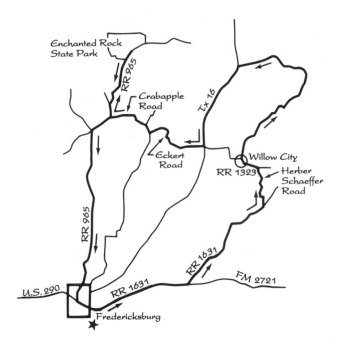

exploring the park, return the way you came, heading south on RR 965 to US 290 and Fredericksburg.

Fredericksburg is a cowboy's Germany. Like New Braunfels, Fredericksburg started as a frontier settlement of German immigrants, and both towns have hung onto and recently rejuvenated their European roots. Until recently, the difference between New Braunfels and Fredericksburg was the difference between a hardware store and a saddle shop, between a wurstfest and a rodeo. In the last few years, Fredericksburg has succumbed to the lure of tourist dollars and vices, allowing the development of cutesy boutiques. But just a block off Main Street, the town still retains plenty of that frontier feeling.

The citizens of Fredericksburg have long taken pride in their heritage and have worked to preserve and restore a great many nineteenth-century buildings. Find out more at the **visitors' center,** 101 Pioneer Plaza. The staff will point you to the historic **Vereins Kirche,** a replica of the first public building in Fredericksburg, a combination meeting hall and nondenominational church. It is now a local history archive. The **Pioneer Memorial Museum,** a few blocks west on Main Street, showcases a collection of vernacular buildings from a hundred years ago. Walking tour brochures will take you to the broad backstreets to view Sunday houses, so called because in outlying areas farmers traditionally came into town on Saturday afternoon for shopping and to spend the night so they could attend church services on Sunday. They would spend one night a week in these tiny, two-story cottages.

There are several noteworthy restaurants in Fredericksburg, namely **Altdorf Biergarten & Restaurant,** 301 West Main Street and Orange Street, (210) 997-7774; **Friedhelm's Bavarian Inn,** 905 West Main Street, (210) 997-7024; **Old German Bakery & Restaurant,** 225 West Main Street, (210) 997-9084; and **Fenner & Beans,** 204 East Main Street, (210) 997-2617.

This loop takes you north of Fredericksburg to highland ranches far from river valleys. There are some good hills as you pass the **Cave Creek** community. At 1743-feet elevation, Fredericksburg is the highest town of any size in the Hill Country. You gradually gain even more elevation as you head north from town. Be sure to watch for your left turn onto Herber Schaefer Road about 4 miles beyond the church at Cave Creek. It may be unmarked, but it's the only paved road off to the left. Herber Schaefer Road cuts right through a private ranch with livestock moving about. You'll cross eight cattle guards on this 3-mile stretch of road. That must be a record!

A note on crossing cattle guards: If the cattle guard looks smooth (i.e., it is set at the same height as the road surface, not raised above it), the best thing to do is to ride across at regular speed without braking, keeping your wheels perpendicular to the bars. Going very slowly decreases your stability on the cattle guard and might cause you to swerve—not good. Sometimes, the faster you go, the smoother the crossing. On the other hand, some inexperienced riders get off and walk. If you decide to walk it, don't turn an ankle! You'll have to be the judge at each cattle guard you encounter.

Willow City is no city at all. It's barely a settlement these days. Sometimes a very basic store is open just beyond the Willow City Loop turnoff. The Willow City Loop has become quite a tourist attraction itself recently, partly due to its spectacular scenery and partly due to its abundance of bluebonnets in April. But unless you ride the loop on a weekend in the spring, the loop's character hasn't changed at all. It still feels like a well-hidden secret. The loop is a regular Gillespie County road that leads to a few out-of-the-way ranches and meets up with TX 16. Along this 13-mile road, you'll have a great downhill and some amazing vistas. You'll cross creekbeds that are almost always dry or nearly dry. And you'll notice that the world changes. . . . Gone are the familiar limestone cliffs of the Hill County you may be familiar with. The hills and creekbeds are made of crystalline pink granite. These are the southernmost reaches of the Llano Uplift, which covers much of Llano County and the upper Highland Lakes areas. Apparently, bluebonnets prefer the soils associated with these granite outcroppings because this is the part of the Hill Country where they bloom the most. Depending on the winter's weather, the bluebonnets along the Willow City Loop and TX 16 often blanket the roadsides.

Eckert Road has another of the world's finest collections of cattle guards on the way to Rabke's and Crabapple Road. Rabke's Table Ready Meats is a favorite with cyclists attending the Kerrville Easter Weekend Rally. The turkey sandwiches are fantastic, and the beef jerky and turkey jerky, supposedly, can't be beat. Rabke's makes a perfect snack stop on this long ride without other stores. Before you start your ride, call ahead to be sure they'll be open: (210) 685-3266.

After crossing Crabapple Creek just beyond Rabke's, you'll follow Crabapple Road, which again goes through private ranch property with loose livestock. Watch for cows—and for cow patties! Crabapple leads past the forlorn buildings of the Crabapple community, including a lonely, old church.

Just as you get on RR 965 North, you'll see the handsome **Welgehausen Ranch** on the left. These are some of the most photographed old limestone ranch buildings around. As you crest the rise from Crabapple Creek a few miles further, you'll see **Enchanted Rock** for the first time. This is one of the greatest views in the Hill Country. The "rock" at first looks smaller than you might expect, but it is still 3 miles away. Enchanted Rock is the second largest exposed batholith in the United States, after Stone Mountain in Georgia. It is a smooth, bald dome of pink granite, but it has small fissures in the rock that reportedly make strange noises when they expand or contract due to rapid drops or rises in temperature—usually occurring at sunrise or sunset or as a sudden cold front passes. The Native Americans living in the area heard these noises and decided that the rock was haunted by spirits. Thus it was named, "Enchanted Rock." The pink and gray granite used to be molten igneous rock, and that's why it looks as if it flowed into its current shape.

The 1,643-acre park has hiking trails around the base of the rock and neighboring **Turkey Peak** to the east and **Little Rock** to the west, another even craggier giant. You can take any path you want to the top. Rubber-soled touring shoes will work fine. The round-trip hike takes little more than an hour. The steepest routes are on the north side, where technical climbers scale what the rest of us can't. I especially enjoy Enchanted Rock in the fall. Late October and early November are fine times to ride here.

The route back to Fredericksburg is simple. Head south on RR 965 all the way, though with a county map, you'll discover some other options. All of the roads in this area are a real treat. As you climb south from Crabapple Creek on RR 965, you'll ride across one of the highest plateaus in the Hill Country with elevations right at 2000 feet. A few miles north of town, just beyond a picnic area, you'll see an old, abandoned granite quarry, similar to the one near Marble Falls, where stone used to build the state capitol building in Austin was gathered. There used to be a huge balanced rock just a short walk from the picnic area here, but several years ago, some pranksters dynamited the rock and put an end to a curiosity of erosion that had lasted for thousands of years.

One last sidetrip before you get back to your own Sunday house: consider taking a right turn at the sign to **Cross Mountain.** It's just a short way up to get a fine view of Fredericksburg from a hawk's perspective.

ACCOMMODATIONS: Peachtree Inn, 401 South Washington (US 87 South), Fredericksburg, (210) 997-2117. **Sunset Motel,** 900 Adams Street (TX 16 South), Fredericksburg, (210) 997-9581. To find a bed and breakfast call the two locator services: **Bed & Breakfast of Fredericksburg,** at (210) 997-4712, and **Be My Guest Lodging,** at (210) 997-7227.

CAMPING: Lady Bird Johnson Municipal Park, 3 miles south on TX 16 South, (210) 997-4202. **Enchanted Rock State Park,** 17 miles north on RR 965 North, (915) 247-3903.

FOR MORE INFORMATION: Fredericksburg Chamber of Commerce, 101 Pioneer Plaza, Fredericksburg, Texas, 78624, (210) 997-6523.

LOCAL BIKE SHOP: Closest shop is **Bicycles, Etc.,** at 1412 Broadway (TX 27 East), 25 miles southwest in Kerrville, (210) 896-6864.

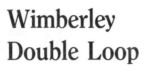

Wimberley
Double Loop

Having two loops out of **Wimberley** allows you to customize your ride. Each loop is exactly 30 miles and each loop starts and ends at the same spot, the square in Wimberley, which is just east of **Cypress Creek.** So you might ride one loop in the morning, return to Wimberley for lunch or a swim, and ride the other loop in the afternoon. The southern loop climbs to the **Devil's Backbone** with fantastic views from high above the **Blanco Valley.** The northern loop climbs to **Driftwood** and takes in some lovely hills along upper **Onion Creek.**

The southern loop to Fischer begins at the square in Wimberley, heading south on RR 12 toward San Marcos. After climbing Devil's Backbone on RR 12, turn right on RR 32 for 12 miles along the backbone ridge. Turn right on FR 484 and continue two-tenths of a mile to **Fischer** and then turn right again onto Fischer Store Road just before the old **Fischer Store.** Fischer Store Road becomes Hays County 181 and crosses the **Blanco River.** Continue on Hays 181 another 5.5 miles. Hays 181 ends at FM 2325 (not marked at this intersection). Turn right on FM 2325 and ride 3.9 miles back to RR 12 and Wimberley.

- **Starting point:** Wimberley (for both loops)
- **Route:** loop one—Wimberley to Fischer
  loop two—Wimberley to Driftwood
- **Mileage:** loop one—30 miles
  loop two—30 miles
- **Terrain:** Several challenging hills on both of these loops.
- **Best time to ride:** Anytime of the year the weather permits. Sundays are better than Saturdays.
- **Traffic conditions:** Heavy traffic on RR 12 South, moderate to very light traffic on the remainder of the routes.
- **Road conditions:** Good RR and FM roads, but the county roads can be quite rough, especially Hays County 181 on the Devil's Backbone loop.

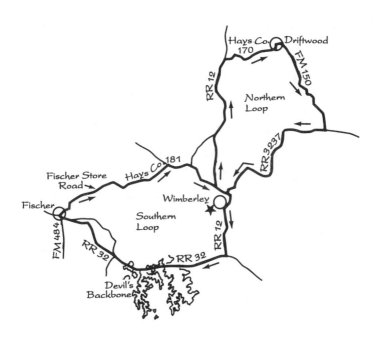

The northern loop to Driftwood begins at the square in Wimberley, heading north on RR 12 toward **Dripping Springs.** After 8.8 miles, turn right on Hays County Road 170 (watch for it where RR 12 is wide). Hays County 170 ends at the old **Driftwood Store** (now an antiques shop, open on weekends). Turn right (south) onto FM 150 (unmarked here) toward **Kyle.** FM 150 meets RR 3237 6.4 miles later. Turn right on RR 3237 to RR 12. Turn right on RR 12 to return to the square.

Wimberley has long been a mecca for Houstonites escaping the heat and humidity of the coast. And like Fredericksburg, Wimberley in recent years seems to have attracted more than its share of touristy boutiques. But it also has several cafés that are especially good, and it's on Cypress Creek and an easily accessible stretch of the Blanco River. No other town in Texas has so many cypress trees. Each October, Wimberley hosts one of Texas' best organized and most scenic century rides, the Wimberley Hillaceous Hundred. The two loops I have created for you show off some of the best of the Hillaceous Hundred route.

It is difficult to say which is the tougher of the two. The climb to the Devil's Backbone on RR 12 south of town is infamous among cyclists, but as much of its notoriety comes from the devilish name as from the climb itself. True, it is a mile-and-a-half-long grind to get to the top. But once there, the top of the ridge rolls west rather gently. The northern loop probably climbs as much as the southern route. It's just that the views are not as spectacular. The really joyous stretch of the northern loop is RR 150 southeast of Driftwood as the road crosses Onion Creek. So, sooner or later, if not on the same day, try both loops. And after you've done them in one direction (they are both described in clockwise direction in this guide), come back and do them again in the other direction. I never tire of these roads. The Wimberley area is indeed "hillaceous," but hillaceous is wonderful.

LOOP ONE: Wimberley to Fischer

The **Blanco River** starts 20 miles west of Blanco or about 45 miles west of Wimberley. As you leave town on RR 12, you'll cross the shallow Blanco and you'll be able to see why the river got its name (blanco is Spanish for white). The riverbed is solid limestone, and is very close to white under a foot or two of clear water. No other Hill Country river has such a consistently wide and smooth bed. It is a fun river to wade in.

Halfway up the, shall we say, noticeable climb to the Backbone, you enter the **Edwards Aquifer Recharge Zone.** That means that the area is particularly important to the movement of surface water down into the porous rock hundreds of feet below, where it moves in a mysterious underground river system. That water eventually comes back to the surface as springwater, and much of it is pumped to the surface for the municipal water supplies of San Marcos, New Braunfels, and San Antonio. This environmentally sensitive zone stretches for many miles from near Austin southwest to **Hondo.**

Atop the Devil's Backbone, there are stores at the intersection with RR 32 and farther along in the settlement of Devil's Backbone around the **Devil's Backbone Tavern,** one of the better places to have a beer halfway through a bike ride. Note that the tavern is the last store along this loop. There is nothing else until you get back to Wimberley—so fill your water bottles with water!

Take snacks to the picnic area on the right about a mile beyond the tavern. These views are as distant as you can get in the Hill Country. You can see about 20 miles to the north. The precipitous views end a mile or so after the picnic area, though you remain high above the land on either side. Out of sight to the south is **Canyon Lake** while the Blanco, hidden in the trees, parallels the Backbone to the north.

It used to be that the Fischer Store was one of the great old general stores still surviving, full of dusty hardware and ice-cold Cokes in little bottles. But the Fischer Store has finally passed away. The silvery-gray, galvanized tin building stands about as solidly as ever, but all that remains inside is a small post office. Fischer Store Road is a quiet backroad that travels through lovely ranches and down to an attention-getting bridge over the Blanco far below. The road can be quite bumpy and full of potholes in places, especially in Hays County where the road is called Hays County 181. Conditions may change year to year and season to season. Those of you riding on racer-thin tires may want to tread lightly here. Beefier tires are highly recommended. But it is roads like this one that still make the Hill Country so fun to explore. You usually have the road to yourself, and the experience is peaceful and memorable.

LOOP TWO: Wimberley to Driftwood

Starting on RR 12 North, you'll see that it does not climb as suddenly as it does to the south, but it still climbs. Wimberley is only a little over 800 feet above sea level while the surrounding hills in every direction range from twelve-hundred to a bit over fourteen-hundred feet. The highest points in the area are **Big Head Mountain** (1473 feet) just west of Fischer and **Lone Man Mountain** (1421 feet) just east of RR 12 and about 8 miles north of Wimberley.

First heights, now depths. You will pass **Woodcreek Resort** while heading north on RR 12. Woodcreek property protects one of the most notorious underground water caverns in the Hill Country— **Jacob's Well.** The well is a cave full of water. To go spelunking there, you'd need an aqualung. But because of six deaths down below in the hidden passageways, Jacob's Well is strictly off limits to idle thrillseekers.

The old general store in Driftwood is now the Driftwood Country Store, an antiques and collectibles shop only open on the weekends. It lacks the lonely resonance of the empty Fischer Store, but at least it's alive. Just 2 miles north of Driftwood, off our route, is **Salt Lick Bar B Que,** across RR 1826 from **Camp Ben McCulloch.** Consistently considered one of the best barbecue joints in the state, the Salt Lick serves up a unique blend of southern and Hawaiian spices.

Back on the route heading south, wonderful FM 150 crosses Onion Creek several times with a good climb after each crossing. For your efforts, there is a store at the T intersection with RR 3237, which is the road back to Wimberley. A few miles from the store, don't miss **St. Stephens Church** tucked back in the trees on the left. The church is relatively new, but it was built in the style of the more modest Spanish churches of colonial times, using a handsome native limestone. The church is a nice place to take a final break before rolling down into Wimberley to rest.

If you're looking for somewhere to eat in town, try any of these three possibilities: **Cypress Creek Café,** on the square, (512) 847-2515; **John Henry's,** on the square, (512) 847-5467; and **Mr. Mike's Le Buffet,** on RR 12 North, (512) 847-2009.

ACCOMMODATIONS: Mountain View Motel, RR 12 South (about 3 miles from town), Wimberley, (512) 847-2992. **Rio Bonito Resort** (rustic cottages), RR 12 South, Wimberley, (512) 847-2232. **Singing Cypress Gardens** (bed and breakfast), Mill Race Lane, Wimberley (512) 847-9344. Other options are to stay in New Braunfels for both the New Braunfels and Wimberley rides or to stay in Austin or San Marcos.

CAMPING: Blue Hole Campground, north off Old Kyle Road just east of central Wimberley, (512) 847-9127.

FOR MORE INFORMATION: Wimberley Chamber of Commerce, on Ranch Road 12 (across from the bank), Wimberley, Texas, 78676, (512) 847-2201.

LOCAL BIKE SHOP: Closest shop is **Freewheeling** at 230 North LBJ, 15 miles east in San Marcos, (512) 392-9514.

The Kerrville-Bandera-Leakey Loop Tour

In an area so beautiful and so suited to cycling as the Texas Hill Country, it is tough to choose one multiday route. The day rides described in this chapter would all make fine legs of a multiday loop. New Braunfels, **Marble Falls, Blanco,** Wimberley, and Fredericksburg are each good places to begin and end a loop tour. But, in the end **Kerrville** wins out. Kerrville is, as they say, "in the heart of the hills." The town is not as charming as Fredericksburg or Wimberley, but Kerrville makes a great base from which to start because it has plenty of services—motels and restaurants galore, and a state park, too. Kerrville truly is at the crossroads of the Hill Country. Plus, Kerrville has a bike shop for those last-minute adjustments, accessories, and the inevitable paraphernalia each of us seems to crave right before we set out on a multiday trek.

- **Starting point:** Kerrville (loop)
- **Route:** day one—Kerrville to Bandera
  day two—Bandera to Garner State Park
  day three—Garner State Park to Lost Maples State Natural Area
  day four—Lost Maples State Natural Area to Kerrville
- **Mileage:** day one—40 miles
  day two—50 miles
  day three—34 miles
  day four—47 miles
  total—171 miles
- **Terrain:** Gently rolling to hilly with moderate to steep climbs and a few flat stretches.
- **Best time to ride:** late March to late May and late September to late November
- **Traffic conditions:** Heavy in Kerrville and Bandera and some trucks on US 83, but otherwise light.
- **Road conditions:** Good, well-paved roads, though some are without shoulders. TX 39 is narrow; US 83 and TX 27 have shoulders.

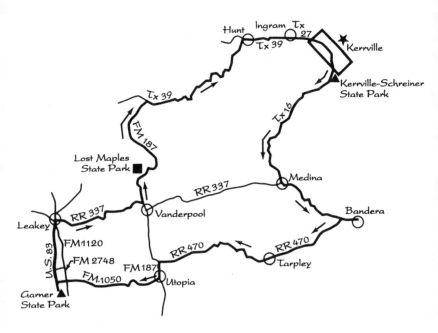

If I wanted to explore the Hill Country on a ride from place to place to place (a REAL tour), and I had just four days, this is the ride I would do. It includes some of the best scenery and some of the toughest climbs in the Hill Country. After all, climbing and descending real hills is the reason we ride here. If you're coming to the Hill Country, you might as well find out about those **Leakey** killer hills! And as a bonus, this loop tour passes through some of the region's quaintest burgs along some of its quietest roads and precious rivers. There are several options for camping and motels, though, to keep the days under 60 miles, you'll probably opt to camp at least one if not two nights. But that's great, because you'll find some of Texas' loveliest state parks along the way—with cool views and hot showers! So get those last-minute knick-knacks for your bike, pack your bags, and let's roll on one of the state's greatest rides.

The Kerrville-Bandera-Leakey Loop Tour heads south and west of Kerrville, winding down through delightful river valleys and over the steep ridges in between. The best times of the year to ride this loop are late March to late May and late September through late November. Spring wildflowers peak about mid-April, though various flowers bloom at different times, depending on seasonal fluctuations, between March and early June. In the fall, a rare treat of New Englandlike color awaits you at **Lost Maples State Natural Area** near **Vanderpool.** The maples turn brilliant red and orange for a few weeks between late October and mid-November. Call the park in early October to find out exactly when the leaves are expected to reach their peak in color.

DAY ONE: Kerrville to Bandera

With a population of about 18,000, Kerrville is by far the largest town in the Hill Country west of I-35. (It even has a mall!) This fast-growing town is home to many retirees who believed *Reader's Digest* when it suggested years ago that Kerrville had a nearly ideal climate. And at one time, Kerr County boasted more millionaires per capita than any other county in the United States, mostly due to the handsome ranches (also known as tax shelters) and dude retreats that cover the area. Kerrville is also the heart of Texas' summer camp country. Dozens of camps in the hills to the east, south, and especially to the west up the Guadalupe River, draw thousands of kids from Texas and beyond every summer—a good reason to avoid riding around Kerrville during July and August. Those big ranches, such as the huge **Y.O. Ranch** near **Mountain Home,** attract hunters of native white-tailed deer and more exotic species imported from Africa, especially in the fall, but except for the banners welcoming the hunters to town—and the sudden proliferation of gun racks in pick-up truck windows—they usually go unnoticed.

Kerrville's greatest attraction is the landscape that surrounds it—the river valleys and hills that you'll explore on this tour. Kerrville's second best attraction is the one and only **Cowboy Artists of America Museum.** The Cowboy Artists of America group is a tightly knit club, and membership is exclusive. You have to paint in the style of Remington or Russell or both, or at least act like you do, and you have to have gotten pretty darn rich off of what you sell. But the museum is a lovely, modern creation set among ten acres of oak trees just southeast of town, and is open to everyone, Russell devotees and Remington greenhorns alike. Check it out at 1550 Bandera Highway, or call (512) 896-2553.

For a more old-fashioned and less pretentious museum experience, drop by the **Hill Country Museum** in the old **Schreiner Mansion** next to the main post office downtown, at 226 Earl Garrett Street. The Schreiners used to own just about everything in Kerrville—the bank, the department store, the college, the land—and this museum puts them in their place as the kings of Kerrville commerce. The mansion is on the National Register of Historic Places. Call (512) 896-8633 for more information.

You'll probably begin this tour wherever you park your car in Kerrville. Most motels make a good base if you are staying at the same one before and after the tour, but be sure to ask. Note that **Kerrville-Schreiner State Park** does not allow vehicles to be left unattended on days you are not camping there. Beyond the outskirts of Kerrville, **Medina** is the only place you will find a store along today's route, so carry full water bottles and ample snacks with you.

As you head south from Kerrville on TX 16, you'll be traveling the prettiest part of the longest state highway in Texas. You'll climb out of the Guadalupe River Valley past **Quiet Valley Ranch,** home of the famous **Kerrville Folk Festival,** to a climb that is famous (or infamous) with cyclists from around the state—**Eagle's Nest,** above the headwaters of **Turtle Creek.** There is no sign marking the top of the climb, but look for the old "Swiss-cheese" limestone house on the right side of the road above a big rock wall in a cluster of huge cedar trees. That's Eagle's Nest. Watch out for the tight turns on the descent to Robinson Creek and be careful. TX 16 is supremely graceful as it follows the **Medina River** into Medina. There are a few river crossings that make great spots for taking a break and a dip. In this part of the Hill Country, it is especially easy to spot the course of a creek or river by looking for the path of tall cypress trees that line its banks.

The tiny town of Medina saw busier days when residents of San Antonio used to take a weekend drive to the old cottages along the river. But Jeep Collins still manufactures ladies' handbags here, and Medina is trying to make a comeback as the apple capital of Texas. Look for a few apple boutiques along TX 16 that also sell baked goods, Texas pecans, and other desserts and delicacies. The apple harvest begins in late August and lasts through September, so if you are an apple fan, that's a good time to visit. There is a modest store where TX 16 meets RR 337, and Medina sometimes has a café, but sometimes not.

Between Medina and **Bandera,** TX 16 winds along the Medina River, crossing it several times. This section of the ride rolls only slightly. For the afternoon, you get the luxury of being surrounded by craggy hills without going over them.

Bandera calls itself the "Cowboy Capital of the World," and it seems there are a lot more cowboys in the Hill Country than there are apples. Bandera has been a dude ranch haven for decades, including the **Dixie** and the **Mayan,** but lately, the town has become known for its professional racetrack, **Bandera Downs,** a few miles east of town (beyond our route) on TX 16. Seasonal rodeos are also a main draw here. Bandera plays up its cowboy culture with a western set downtown, complete with boardwalks and fake-front buildings. To its credit, it is still easier to pick up some hardware and even a good saddle in this town than it is to find a couple of canvasses by one of the cowboy artists of America.

Like Kerrville, Bandera's best tourist attraction is the Hill Country—the Medina River runs by the east side of town. And like Kerrville, Bandera's second best attraction is a museum. But nothing the **Frontier Times Museum** displays could possibly be considered art—cowboy or otherwise—or really even historical. This is a museum full of funk—one of the best $1.50 investments you'll ever make. Where else could you see legendary Texan Judge Roy Bean's discarded bottles, a Texas map made of rattlesnake rattles, a shrunken head from South America, and a two-headed goat? The goat is stuffed, and the rest of the stuff is dusty, but it's the thought that counts. The colorful founder of *Frontier Times Magazine* started this collection of incredible kitsch in 1927. Look for the museum at 506 13th Street at Pecan Street, a block behind the **Bandera County Courthouse.**

Eat at the **OST Restaurant.** The OST, which stands for Old Spanish Trail, serves chuckwagon-style Tex-Mex and chicken-fried mystery meats and has a decent salad bar. It's the culinary heart of this cowboy capital.

DAY TWO: Bandera to Garner State Park

Today, after breakfast at the OST with the other dudes, you'll retrace your steps back on TX 16 for 3 miles past the **Bandera County Fairgrounds** to RR 470 West to **Tarpley.** Turn left on RR 470, and you'll immediately get away from it all—or almost all of it. RR 470 doesn't go much of anywhere, except to Utopia, so you should have the road almost entirely to yourself. As opposed to TX 16, RR 470 spends most of its 30 miles in the high and dry hills just north of the **Balcones Fault,** not down in a creek or river valley. The views are expansive, and the solitude makes for some wonderful cycling.

Some of the highest hills in the area surround Tarpley. Just a few miles before you get to Tarpley, **Chalk Mountain** (1960 feet) and **Sugarloaf Mountain** (1900 feet) will be to your right, while the highest point south, to your left, is **Flag Mountain** (1995 feet).

Tarpley itself is not much more than a combination gas station and store, though that store is a welcomed snack stop along this little frequented leg of the tour. (The Tarpley store is 15 miles from Bandera and 19 miles from Utopia, so carry some snacks with you.) Dinosaur tracks have recently been discovered very near Tarpley. The tracks appear in a layer of limestone that used to be a squishy Pleistocene bog.

You might inquire at the store if you are interested in seeking them out.

There are several good hills west of Tarpley with a few short steep sections. As you descend from these, you'll be coming into the **Sabinal River Valley.** The Sabinal Valley is an idyllic setting, and the town of **Utopia** proves it. Utopia is best known for Utopia Spring Water, pure water taken from several local wells and bottled at a plant on the north side of town. Stop in for a sample. Cyclists know Utopia as a great place to stop for lunch, most notably at the **Lost Maples Inn.** The Inn is not exactly a carbo-loaders dream, but you've been working hard, and their hamburgers are among my favorites anywhere. Daily lunch specials lend variety to the standard café fare. There is a shady yard next to the Lost Maples Inn, and I've seen many a cyclist stretched out there before, during, and after a good lunch. There is usually another café or two in town, but these come and go, so check around to discover a new place. There are a couple of stores and a post office where you can send cards with a Utopia postmark—impress your friends! (They'll be hard-pressed to find Utopia on the map.) Everything in Utopia is on or within a block of FM 187.

As you leave town on FM 1050 West toward **Garner State Park**, **Utopia Park** will be on your right. There are picnic tables under huge cypress trees along the **Sabinal River.** If you'd like to have a picnic, take a dip, or take a nap, this is a good place to do it.

FM 1050 seems a perpetually sunny stretch of road with shady spots only where **Blanket Creek** and **Cherry Creek** cross the road. The short, scrubby oak trees will never get the chance to hang over the road. The sunny, open spaces of FM 1050 give the afternoon's ride a frontier feeling, like you are really lighting out for the West. This is some wild, open country. The land is all private ranches, but the only signs of civilization you see are fences and a few ranch gates. The ubiquitous black buzzards are easy to spot, hovering over any road kill worthy of a scavenger's glance. But you might be on the lookout for red-tailed hawks and roadrunners, even a wild turkey. Strangely enough, for all of their notoriety as Lone Star mascots and road kill staples in this state, you'd be hard-pressed to spot a foraging armadillo. Like raccoons, they come out in the late evening and at night.

There are three handsome climbs along the way before you descend into yet another river valley—your fourth in two days. This time it is the valley of the **Frio River.** Frio is Spanish for cold, and the river can be quite chilly, even in the middle of the summer, because it comes from springs deep underground just a few miles north of Leakey. You will cross the Frio just before you get to US 83. Garner State Park is 1 mile south on US 83.

Garner is one of the most beloved and one of the most popular state parks in Texas—and for good reason. When I was a boy, these hills seemed like mountains to me. Here, the Frio is at its best, ideal for swimming, tubing and lazing about. Garner also offers high cliffs and hidden caves to explore, plus some creature comforts not usually found in Texas state parks—cabins, a dance pavilion on the banks of the Frio River, a snack bar and a camp store in summer, paddle boats on the Frio, even a miniature golf course. (Beware: the deteriorating putting "greens" may be the biggest obstacles to fair play, but the setting, under a grove of immense oak trees, can't be beat.) The 1,420-acre park was named for John Nance "Cactus Jack" Garner, the fiesty vice-president under Franklin Roosevelt, who preceded Harry Truman as vice-president. It was FDR's Civilian Conservation Corps (CCC) program that built the dance pavilion and other park buildings and roadways during the depression in the 1930s. Garner State Park has been a mecca for Texans ever since, especially residents of the San Antonio area, who show up on summer weekends in droves. Plan your stay at Garner for the off-season or a summer weekday.

Because Garner has cabins, it's one of the few state parks non-campers can enjoy. The state park also has screened shelters and hundreds of nice campsites in old pecan groves. Make your reservations early for cabins. There are other rustic accommodations along the Frio north and south of the park. You might consider the **Rio Frio B & B** in **Rio Frio,** where you can also see the state's largest live oak tree. But be sure to spend an afternoon at Garner even if you choose not to stay there.

DAY THREE: Garner State Park to Lost Maples

Take a morning swim or hike at Garner because this is the shortest day of your tour. Lunch in Leakey is only 12 easy miles away. Leaving Garner, you have a choice of routes. U.S. 83 North is not highly trafficked and has a shoulder all the way to Leakey, but I still prefer backtracking a couple of miles on FM 1050 to the east side of the Frio, turning left on FM 2748 to Rio Frio, and continuing north on FM 1120 to Leakey. You'll have these backroads to yourself all the way to town. There is a very nice low-water crossing of the Frio that allows a few inches of water over the road after spring rains and summer thunder-showers. It's another good spot for a dip, but don't try to ride across, even if there are a few inches of water over the road. Take off your shoes and walk your bike. This little diversion makes for a good photo opportunity.

You'll rejoin U.S. 83 just south of the oft-mispronounced town of Leakey. Say "LAY-key," not "LEEK-ee." Leakey is the tiny county seat of Real County. In fact, Real County only has two towns and about 1,200 people. If you are looking for an ambitious side trip that will add a day to your tour, take the ultimate Hill Country loop ride north and west via RR 336, TX 41, RR 335, and RR 337. There are no services until you get to **Barksdale** and **Camp Wood,** 70 miles and 75 miles, respectively, into this challenging century ride, but the roller coaster hills and scenic views make this optional loop worth the effort. (Please do note that, because of the terrain, this may well be the most demanding century ride in the state. Leave a full extra day for this loop, and carry extra water and snacks.)

Leakey itself is a charming town with old limestone buildings, several motels, and a couple of good restaurants. If you decide to stay an extra day here, try the **Welcome Inn.** The **Frio Valley Café** offers acceptable fare, but **The Smokehouse** up the street in a converted Dairy Queen serves the best turkey sandwiches in Texas. Everything at the Smokehouse is produced by Oink, Inc. Pigtail art proliferates. **TJ's,** a modest sandwich dive near the courthouse, offers barbecue and pizza as well. There is even a genuine soda fountain (circa 1960) at **Leakey Drug** across the street. The **Real County Museum** is just behind the courthouse, but in keeping with the laid-back pace here in Leakey, it seems to be closed most of the time.

As you head east from Leakey on RR 337 toward Vanderpool, you'll cross the Frio River for the last time, pass a cedar post mill on the left, and crest a rise that takes you back into the hidden valleys and wild highlands between the Frio River and the Sabinal River. Get ready for two of the most impressive and inspiring climbs in the Hill Country. These are little mini-mountain passes with constant grades of about 5 to 8 percent for a mile or more, sharp curves, rock cuts, and the kind of guardrail dropoffs that can give some level-landers chills. But these are also the kind of climbs that give us Hill Country aficionados thrills and keep us coming back for more. From Leakey, at 1600 feet, you'll climb to over 2000 feet in elevation and drop down about as much to Vanderpool. The first climb comes right after you cross the **Little Dry Frio River,** 6 miles east of Leakey. After you descend to the West Sabinal River, 11 miles from Leakey, you'll climb again. A mile after crossing the Bandera county line, as you begin your final descent into Vanderpool (you'll be flying), you'll find a picnic area on the right that sits high above the valley floor. Take a moment to pause and reflect on your hill-climbing accomplishments. Views like this are rare in Texas. The descent from this picnic area is one of the straightest and steepest in the

Hill Country. Some cyclists brake for comfort and safety, but others go for it. Many a cyclist has set a personal record for top speed on this fast downhill with speeds of 40, 45, and even more than 50 miles per hour. Be careful!

The broad-leafed trees that line the downhills are sycamores, a fast-growing tree planted by the Texas Highway Department to slow erosion. Though hard to capture on film and even in words, from one end to the other, RR 337 is simply a spectacular road.

There is a good general store, the **Lost Maples Store,** with a shady front porch at the intersection of RR 337 and RR 187. It is your last chance to stock up on camping and dinner supplies for the Lost Maples State Natural Area just up the valley.

Lost Maples is a state park with hot showers and the other attractive amenities for which Texas State Parks are known. Its designation as a state natural area declares its purpose as a habitat preserve not only for an isolated (and thus "lost") stand of bigtooth maples, left over from a Pleistocene Ice Age, but also for other rare plants, like American smoketree, Canada moonseed, and witch hazel. There are rare birds from canyon wrens to bald eagles (in winter) and three unique amphibians—the rare barking frog, the Texas salamander, and the Texas cliff frog. The 2,208-acre preserve has 10.5 miles of hiking trails along streambeds and up over steep hills. The headwaters of the Sabinal River are here as well. You might have to have a good pair of hiking boots, a good pair of binoculars, and loads of patience to spot one of the rare species, but I have found Lost Maples to be a likely place for spotting deer and armadillos, animals that are much more common and visible in these parts.

With such a short day (at least in mileage), an afternoon hike is a real possibility. A walk is a good way to keep your climbing thighs limber. Start with the **Maple Trail** just beyond the picnic area, and wander up the Sabinal. The **Visitors' Center** has displays on the area's native and rare flora and fauna. Stop there first. And if you are taking this tour in October or November, when the maples might be turning, you can call the "Maple Hotline" after October 1 to find out when the park rangers expect the colors to peak: 1-800-792-1112.

One safety note: Shortly beyond the Visitors' Center, you'll cross the Sabinal River on a low-water crossing so low it almost always has just enough water flowing over it to make it slick. If it is at all wet, do not ride your bicycle across; walk your bike, using the steps on either side if necessary.

If you need indoor accommodations near Lost Maples, try **Fox Fire Cabins** on the Sabinal in Vanderpool. The Bandera County

Chamber of Commerce can provide the names of other accommodations in the Lost Maples area.

DAY FOUR: Lost Maples to Kerrville

We end our four-day jaunt to the southwestern frontier of the Hill Country with a classic return to Kerrville along the Guadalupe River. You'll cross the Gaudalupe nine times today along one of the loveliest and most serpentine state highways anywhere. There aren't many roads that trace the course of a river as closely as TX 39 follows the Guadalupe. TX 39 is a water snake of a road, gliding gracefully downriver toward home.

But first, there is work to be done. Turning north out of Lost Maples on RR 187, you immediately begin a dramatic climb out of the Sabinal River Valley to a higher and more arid plateau that separates the Sabinal from the Guadalupe. As opposed to the climbs of day three, which finessed their way to the tops of ridges by cutting a steadily angled contour around the hillsides, the climb out of Lost Maples simply blasts straight up. This 1-mile climb is one of the steepest in the state. I'd say it's one of the top five! Even the depth of the rock cut is dramatic. It's like riding in a tilted, man-made canyon. You can be sure this climb wastes no time getting RR 187 out of the Sabinal Valley. Getting yourself out may take a little longer. Just make sure you are juiced up and ready to go.

Notice the uniformity of the trees and plant life on top of the plateau compared to the rich variety of Lost Maples. This shows what a difference surface water and a few hundred feet of elevation can make. The plateau, a piece of the larger **Edwards Plateau,** rolls up and down to the junction with TX 39. Then, as you head east on TX 39, you drop first to a dry wash that is sometimes the south fork of the Guadalupe and at other times a dry riverbed of rocks. But by the next crossing, the river is perennial. I've never seen it dry here. Underground springs feed the stream year-round.

The first half dozen crossings of the Guadalupe are true low-water crossings, just inches or maybe a foot above the water, and surprisingly narrow for a state highway. It used to be that all roads in the Hill Country had crossings this low and narrow (virtually one-lane), but most have been replaced by elevated bridges that remain passable even when the waters rise. Now these crossings along TX 39 are the rare exceptions, and this lends them great charm. At one point when the river is on the left, you might notice the curb of a former roadway that actually ran along the fairly smooth riverbed. Now, that's swimming in the car!

The closer the road gets to **Hunt,** the more resort cottages, fancy homes, and summer camps line the river banks. Most of these date back to the 1930s and 1940s, a few even to the 1920s, when the roads were gravel and only the low-water crossings were cement.

Hunt has a great store, called **The Store.** It is the first store you will have come to since Vanderpool, and it makes a great lunch stop on day four. There is a little café inside that serves French Tacos, Hunt Tacos, and other unique creations. The bathrooms are marked Does and Bucks. (This here's Deer Country.) In fact, you might think that Hunt was named for the verb, to hunt, but actually it wasn't.

After re-entering civilization at Hunt, you'll cross the Guadalupe only two more times. At the second crossing, there is a picnic area on the right and a particularly fine area for wading and swimming in the river. Take advantage of it, for photos, for cooling off, for the fun of it, because the Guadalupe won't be so inviting or so convenient again.

When I was a kid, I used to go dam sliding at **Ingram Dam,** just west of **Ingram.** You'll see the dam on your right. But don't partake of this ancient ritual in bike shorts or even in a good swimsuit. Junker jeans cut-offs are de rigueur. Dam sliding is just that—sliding down the slick spillway on the seat of your pants. It makes for quite a scene in the middle of the summer. Just beyond the dam is the **Point Theater** and the **Hill Country Arts Foundation** where you can learn to paint bluebonnets or, during the summer, catch a hokey production of a Rogers and Hammerstein musical. The artsy-craftsy **Ingram Loop** is just beyond **Johnson Creek.** Turn off of TX 39 for a block here to peruse the antique shops, potters' wares, and a few galleries in what used to be downtown Ingram 70 years ago.

Then it's back to the big city. At Ingram, you join TX 27. There is a shoulder all the way to Kerrville and TX 27 is Kerrville's main street, coming in from the west, so it should not be too hard to get back to where you started. Riding this final stretch from Ingram to Kerrville makes an abrupt but brief (only 7 miles to go) return to traffic and roadside businesses. In contrast with this cluttered finale, remember what it was like having the road to yourself on those wonderful roads to Medina, Bandera, Tarpley, Utopia, Leakey, and Vanderpool. Recall the cool crossings of the Medina, the Sabinal, the Frio, and the Guadalupe. Rejoice in the wide open spaces that still remain on the western frontier of the Texas Hill Country.

ACCOMMODATIONS: The Hillcrest Inn, 1508 Sidney Baker Street (TX 16 North), Kerrville, (210) 896-7400. **The Sands Motel,** 1145 Junction Highway (TX 27 West), Kerrville, (210) 896-5000. **Best West-**

ern Sunday House Inn, 2124 Sidney Baker Street (TX 16 North), Kerrville, (210) 896-1313. **Bed & Breakfast in Kerrville** is a reservation service for local bed and breakfasts, located in **The Now Shop** at 849 Junction Highway; call them at (210) 895-1244. **Riverfront Motel** (a collection of cabins on the Medina River), at the TX 173 bridge, Bandera, (210) 796-3690. **Bandera Inn,** 1900 TX 16 South, Bandera, (210) 796-3093. **Rio Frio B & B,** on FM 1120 (7 miles south of Leakey and 4 miles north of Garner State Park), Rio Frio, (210) 232-6633. **Welcome Inn,** U.S. 83 and 7th Street, Leakey, (210) 232-5246. **Fox Fire** (cabins on the Sabinal River), on RR 187 (just south of Lost Maples Natural Area), Vanderpool, (210) 966-2200.

CAMPING: Kerrville-Schreiner State Park, 3 miles east of Kerrville on TX 173, (210) 257-5392. **Yogi Bear's Jellystone Park,** on the Medina River on the north side of the TX 173 bridge in Bandera, (210) 796-3751. **Garner State Park,** on U.S. 83 (1 mile south of Rio Frio), (210) 232-6132. **Lost Maples Natural Area,** on RR 187 (4 miles north of Vanderpool), (210) 966-3413.

FOR MORE INFORMATION: Kerrville Chamber of Commerce, 1200 Sidney Baker Street, Kerrville, Texas, 78028, (210) 896-1155. **Bandera County Chamber of Commerce,** 503 Main Street, Bandera, Texas, 78003, (210) 796-4312.

LOCAL BIKE SHOP: Bicycles, Etc., 1412 Broadway (TX 27 East), Kerrville, (210) 896-6864. This bike shop, run by friendly proprietor Dick Maudlin, is the only one in the Hill Country proper—so stock up!

North Texas Backroads

• • •

Ed Swan

Grand old country homes, stands of pine trees, ponds, lakes, rolling hills, and miles and miles of peaceful roads await you in North Texas. From Northeast Texas' Caddo Lakes and the cypress-filled bayous to the famous cattle-drive trails in the northwest, the region's landscape and sights are especially diverse. These tours are designed to show you the highlights—the places that make Texas legendary.

North Texas is filled with small Thorton Wilder-esque burgs—like Jefferson, Salado, and Tyler—that offer plenty of quirky curiosities with a Texas twist. For those who want to retreat to a world where the pace of life is slower and historical sites lie around every turn, any one of these tours will be ideal.

The flora and fauna you're likely to see on these rides are also a treat. Courtesy of Lady Bird Johnson and her wildflower-planting programs, an unbelievable assortment of wildflowers carpets the landscape as it does in few other parts of the world. When riding in Northeast Texas look for armadillos, raccoons, and opossums. Throughout North Texas, bird watchers may also see red-tailed hawks, swallowtails, and blue herons as well as many others passing through the region.

While pedaling through the woods and cedar breaks, by the lakes and rivers, and over the rolling hills and plains, you won't have to look far to find genuine Texas fare. Whether it's down-home cookin', fiery Tex-Mex, or unsurpassable barbecue you want after a long ride, it's all here. For cyclists with a healthy appreciation for food, North Texas won't disappoint.

Longview to Jefferson Weekender

If you were to ask me where you could spend the best weekend riding in Texas, outside of the Hill Country, I would recommend this pedal-through-the-pines route. **Jefferson** is one of the best destinations, and **Longview** is one of the most striking and friendly "big" cities in Texas—especially for cyclists. Longview's 150-member Bike Club (LBC) is involved in three big cycling events each year—the Rubicon century in May, the Freeze-Your-Fanny-Fifty in February, and the Texas Chainring Challenge weeklong tour in June. The LBC and the Cystic Fibrosis Weekend Getaway (held in October) use the same area this ride uses—it's that much of a jewel.

If you are a stranger in town, call the club or one of the members (see the Appendices for the club's phone number) and you won't be one for long. Besides the gargantuan task of organizing the events mentioned, the LBC holds regular club rides and acts as an advisory body for other events in the area.

The best place to park your car for the weekend (if you don't call one of the club members and get them to watch it for you) is at Longview High School on the north side of town, near the intersection of Loop 281 and U.S. 259. Park on the north side of the school complex, near the football stadium or the swimming pool center.

- **Starting point:** Longview (loop)
- **Route:** day one—Longview to Jefferson
  day two—Jefferson and environs to Longview
- **Mileage:** day one—40 miles
  day two—46 miles
  total—86 miles
- **Terrain:** rolling hills to flat
- **Best time to ride:** good year-round
- **Traffic conditions:** light with some busy roads
- **Road conditions:** good with shoulders

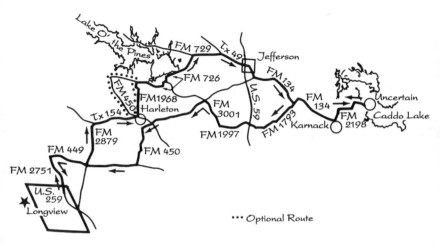

··· Optional Route

The ride begins by heading north on Airline Road (FM 2751). Go 4.9 miles to FM 449 and turn right at the **Gregg County Precinct garage.** Continue to FM 2879 and turn left. By this time, you will have already passed some grand country homes and lots of pine trees. The ponds that adorn the landscape will have you so mesmerized you will have to concentrate to avoid wrecking on the turns.

Once you are 13.4 miles into the ride, turn right on TX 154. At 14 miles there will be a store on your left, but if you ride another 4.8 miles, you will be in **Harleton.** In Harleton, there are stores, restaurants, and bait shops—the home of Texas sushi. Stop at one of the stores near **Lake O' the Pines** and pick up a map of the area. A Dallas company, A.I.D. Associates, Inc., sells maps based on aerial photographs that show every store, dock, town, resort, marina, and park near the lakes with fascinating images and great informational detail. They can be found in most of the Texas lakes' stores or you can order them directly from the company by calling 1-800-AID-MAPS.

Turn left on FM 450 at the store. If you want to cut off about 2 miles, turn left earlier in Harleton on FM 1968. It's not as scenic as FM 450 but it's still nice. Back on FM 450, 22 miles into the trip, turn right on FM 726 (there is a store on the left). Continue on FM 726 until you are 26.7 miles into the trip and veer left at the store on the right.

Prepare yourself for one of the most spectacular views in Texas—Lake O' the Pines. The lake sits to the northwest and the sun sets spectacularly on her. At the end of the spillway, up on the left, are public restrooms and phones. This is a great place to take some pictures of the spillway and enjoy the view.

Once you're back in the saddle, turn right on FM 729 4.9 miles later and go to Highway 49 where you'll turn right. Ride on the good shoulder and be prepared to see some traffic as you come into Jefferson. In another 5.4 miles, you'll pass the **Blackburn Syrup Works** just before entering town. Stop by if you want to see the tin buckets of sweet stuff that sit on every biscuit-laden breakfast table in East Texas. Cross Highway 59 and continue on into town. Turn right on Polk Street 1.9 miles later and go a dozen or so blocks into downtown Jefferson.

Several entire books have been written about the history of Jefferson. In a thumbnail sketch, here's the town's story: It became the western terminus of paddlewheeler streamship traffic that came up from the Gulf on the Red River to Caddo Lake and through the Cypress Bayou into Jefferson. Here cotton was loaded, goods intended for the west were unloaded, and then the boats returned. This changed when dynamite was discovered in the Civil War and the log jam on the Red River that raised the water level and made Jefferson accessible to the big boats was blown up in 1883. The water level immediately dropped 20 feet and Jefferson was left high and dry.

Due to the competition from the steamboat traffic represented, the railroads avoided Jefferson. The end result of all of this was that Jefferson became a prosperous town for almost a century while the unchecked advancement of "progress" robbed most other East Texas towns of commerce and development. The town reached a population of 35,000 residents at its peak and had Texas' first artificial gaslights and ice manufacturing.

Now Jefferson is the bed and breakfast capital of Texas. Antique and curiosity shops are on every corner and its bed and breakfasts are legendary for offering some of the best care and food to be found. All this in a town that still does not lock its doors at night.

Be sure and set aside some time to walk or ride all over the town. Elegant reconstructed mansions are around every corner, and many offer tours. There are at least 60 showplace homes and over 100 points of historical interest in town. Don't plan to leave too early the next day.

Due to the competition, almost all of the restaurants in town are great. If they weren't, they wouldn't last long. Check out the **Bayou Riverboat** tours across the bayou on Polk Street at **Jefferson Riverboat Landing & Depot,** where you'll get all the history you can stand. There is also the **Jefferson and Cypress Bayou Steam Train** that offers rides as well as horse-driven trams that give talking history tours and go all over town.

Book your overnight as soon as you can because rooms fill up quickly all year round. The elegant **Excelsior House Hotel** in the middle of town is the most popular and is often filled more than a year in advance. But there are probably more rooms available in town per population than any other place in the state. Check with the bed and breakfast central reservation number by calling 1-800-JEFF-BNB or **Book-a-Bed-Ahead** at 1-800-345-4044. The Chamber of Commerce can be reached at (903) 665-2672.

If you wanted to do the ride in one day, you could return by heading out of town on Polk Street, over the bayou, and veering right on FM 2208. Take FM 2208 all the way to Highway 154, turn left back toward Harleton, and then repeat the first part of the route from the 19-mile mark back. The return trip would be less than 40 miles for an 80-mile day total. Those looking for less than an 80-mile day could turn back on FM 3001 near the Lake O' the Pines spillway. That would make it about a 40-mile day, but you would miss the lake and Jefferson. If you only have one day, ride the entire day-one route and get a ride back. Don't miss Jefferson.

DAY TWO: Jefferson and Environs to Longview

You can head out Polk Street and do the 40-mile (or less) return described earlier, or go for a slightly longer ride back. The benefits to the longer ride? You get to see **Caddo Lake,** the largest and only natural lake in Texas. The cypress knobs ("knees") rising out of the mists and the moss that cloak the trees make it a pinnacle of natural atmosphere. No one is allowed on the lake without a guide. Experienced boaters get lost in no time, mesmerized by the sameness of the shoreline, which seems to change before your eyes.

Head out of town on Polk Street but go left on FM 134 and at 7.1 miles you will be at FM 1793 where you can take a right and head on back, bypassing Caddo Lake. Or you can continue on 134 (which you will have to double back on once you leave the lake) to **Karnack,** where there are stores. Near the intersection of FM 134 and FM 43 is **Caddo Lake State Park,** worth a view, or a possible place to camp if accommodations in Jefferson are too costly for your liking. To see the lake and get the unique experience of being in **Uncertain,** take FM 2198 to the left and head east for the lake.

Once you have finished gazing at the dark and beautiful realm of Caddo Lake, double back on the same roads to the FM 1793 and FM 134 intersection. The entire side trip was 18 miles; to continue on to Karnack would only be 8 miles round trip. Continue on FM 1793 after the FM 134 T intersection and go 4.8 miles to an unmarked county road and head right for **Woodlawn.** If you miss it just take any of the next right turns to Highway 59, and head up the shoulder to Woodlawn, where there are stores. Load up there because you won't have another chance until you're in Harleton.

Get on FM 1997 which, once you have ridden a total of 17.9 miles, becomes FM 3001. Go 4.3 more miles to FM 2008 and turn left. Then it's on to cross Highway 154 7.1 miles later. Turn right if you need to go the 1.4 miles into Harleton, otherwise continue on to FM 450, which is 30.5 miles into the trip, and turn left. After that turn right on FM 449 4.5 miles later, pass a store in another 3.1 miles, and cross FM 2879 in 3 more miles. Continue on and turn left on FM 2751, which puts you back at the beginning of the previous day's route, 5 miles from your car.

When you do this ride for the first time you get to enjoy Longview, make some new riding friends, see the green vales and pine canyons, experience Jefferson, and bring it all home with you . . . . I really envy you.

ACCOMMODATIONS: To find the bed and breakfast in Jefferson that best suits you, call the bed and breakfast central reservation number, 1-800-JEFF-BNB, or **Book-a-Bed-Ahead** at 1-800-345-4044. **Guest Inn,** 419 Spur 63, Longview, (903) 757-0500. **Holiday Inn,** 3119 Estes Parkway, Longview, (903) 758-0700.

CAMPING: Caddo Lake State Park, off of FM 134 (just north of Karnack), (903) 679-3551. **Lake O' the Pines,** on FM 726 (just west of Jefferson), Longview, (903) 665-2336.

FOR MORE INFORMATION: Longview Chamber of Commerce, P.O. Box 472, Longview, Texas, 75606, (903) 237-4000. **Jefferson Chamber of Commerce,** 116 West Austin Street, Jefferson, Texas, 75675 (903) 665-2672.

LOCAL BIKE SHOPS: Wooley G's, 917 West Loop 281, Longview, (903) 759-2453. **Bike Express,** 1300 Reel Road, Longview, (903) 759-8220.

The Salado
Loop

In spite of all of Salado's exclusive shops, peddling unsur-
passed goods, bed and breakfasts that date back to the
Chisholm Trail days, and historic details that drip from every corner, my
strongest memory of this little town comes from an eerie midnight on
Salado Creek.

The creek, clear and cold enough to be stocked with trout
occasionally, runs through town, bordered by long, flat grassy banks.
Next to it is a statue of the mermaid of Salado, a maiden that was supposedly seen in the creek in a forgotten time. She now stands guard,
lighted at night, over the springs.

I arrived in town at midnight and drove to the creek. A low-
lying mist had shrouded the statue. I walked down to the pool that she
overlooked, and there in the indigo night, I swear I could almost detect
life in the achingly beautiful face shrouded by vapors. Such is the attraction of Salado Creek, which has drawn travelers and Native Americans
into its mystical mists since stagecoach days and even before. Interestingly enough, *salado* means salty, which the freshwater creek is not.
Many believe that cartographers mixed up Salado with the **Lampasas
River,** which is made up of alkaline liquid, and misnamed the creek.

A college thrived here until 1886, and now the ruins stand
guard over the historic village. One continuous connection with the
past that has always made it necessary to pass through **Salado** is the
Stagecoach Inn. Originally named the Shady Villa Inn, its registers list
all the Old West dime-novel names of past guests. Years ago it fell into
disrepair and was revived with the building of a new motel in the back in

- **Starting point:** Salado (loop)
- **Mileage:** 37 miles (with one shorter option and several longer
  options)
- **Terrain:** flat
- **Best time to ride:** year-round
- **Traffic conditions:** light
- **Road conditions:** good

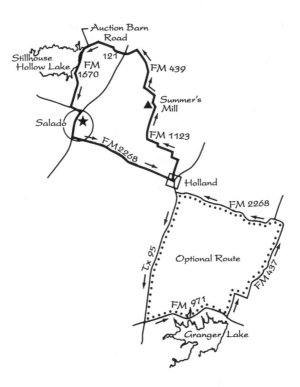

the '40s. It is now an enormous facility with eighty-three modern units in addition to the old inn on Main Street, which serves huge stick-to-your-ribs meals.

Tyler House, down the street, offers dining elegance and eats as good as you've ever tasted. You really can't go wrong in any of Salado's restaurants, bed and breakfasts, or shops. I come to Salado to do a lot of my gift shopping because I can find things here that I have never found anywhere else. In fact, the goods in Salado's shops are unique enough to draw Texans from all over to see what the artisans and shop-keepers have to offer.

There are 130 businesses in this town of 1,200 people, and most of them are curiosity, art, craft, and antique shops. Salado also has twenty-three Texas Historical Markers and eighteen buildings listed on the National Register of Historic Places. Of particular interest are the **Central Texas Area Museum** (817-947-5232) and the **Robertson's Home and Plantation** (817-947-5613). The town even has a Scottish Gathering of the Clans in November, and it's all in a town where they don't have to lock the doors.

The riding here is quiet, easy, and flat. This would have to be the most accessible tour in this book for beginners. The town offers plenty for families to do when not riding. The roads are wide open and almost every cut-through you see turning off of the route goes through to a parallel road on the rectangular route, so you can add or cut off miles as you wish. For example, off of FM 2268 on the way out of Salado toward **Holland,** you can take Krause Road to FM 1123. You'll cut off a few miles and still won't miss the Kodak moment of the whole trip, **Summers' Mill.**

Quiet country roads, four-star dining, a picturesque town with wonderful shops, and a haunting creek . . . it's almost too good to be true. Just wait until you see the roads and the views on this golden route.

Start on the only street in Salado, Main Street, and head south to FM 2268. On the way, turn left on College Hill Road, just out of town, and enjoy the country lane and its view. Go right when you get back on Main Street, which is also FM 2268. At .9 mile turn left on FM 2268. You will ride 10 peaceful, easy, and uninterrupted miles to Holland. In Holland, turn left on FM 1123. You can turn right to go into downtown, where there are restaurants and stores. It is more than 14 miles to the next store.

Follow FM 1123 through some right-angle curves. Ride another 8.8 miles and at 18.8 miles you will pass one of the most picturesque views you'll ever see—the low-water crossing just below the spillway at Summers' Mill. It is a scene quaint enough to be found in a New England hollow.

Stay on FM 1123 (you should be 12.8 miles from Holland and 22.8 miles into the ride now), to FM 439, where you will go left toward **Belton.** Ride another 1.5 miles and you will hit the outskirts of Belton, where there are stores at the turn. If you don't need to stop here, continue on into town for other food choices.

Turn left on Loop 121 and continue on over I-35. At 25.4 miles, **Bell County Expo Center** and its chrome dome will be on your left. At this point you can take the access road for I-35, which follows the interstate the whole 8 miles back to Salado (for a short 33-mile route). If you can make it, continue on because the views to come are even more spectacular.

Go 1.3 miles from I-35, at 26.7 miles, on a curve to the left, take Auction Barn Road, a scenic alternative to continuing on to busy Highway 190. This will take you 1.7 miles to FM 1670, where you turn left at 28.4 miles into the tour.

Prepare yourself for a killer view. Without having to suffer your way over any real hills, you will come upon the spillway to **Stillhouse Hollow Lake,** about a mile down the road. Created when the Brazos

River Authority dammed the Lampasas River in 1968, the lake has a great park, camping, and lots of memorable views. There are phones and bathrooms at the overlook near the entrance to the spillway. Don't miss this, even if you have to drive out to it.

Continue over the spillway and further for 4.9 miles on FM 1670 to FM 2484/FM 1670, where you go left. One more mile and you are back on the I-35 access just north of Salado. Cross over and get back on FM 2268 and head on into the historic town for a total of 37.2 rewarding miles.

Those looking for extra distance can add some miles at Holland by going right (south) on Highway 95 and then turning left on FM 971 to **Granger Lake,** by taking backroads to **Davilla,** and then taking FM 437 and FM 2268 back to Holland for an additional 40 miles. Or you can add miles on at the end by turning right on FM 2484 toward **Youngsport** to FM 440, continuing on to **Florence** and returning to Salado on FM 2843. This is a more hilly route that adds an extra 50 miles. You can cut across almost any of the roads that zig-zag this farmland, adding a block of miles to suit yourself.

Whether you camp, shop, hole up in a bed and breakfast, fish at Stillhouse Hollow Lake, or ride any number of miles, Salado is bound to be a wonderful smalltown experience. While you are there, check out that mermaid and let me know if she winks at you too.

ACCOMMODATIONS: Stagecoach Inn, #1 Main Street, Salado, (817) 947-5111. **Inn on the Creek Bed & Breakfast,** Center Circle, Salado, (817) 947-5554. **The Rose Mansion Bed & Breakfast,** One Rose Way in Victorian Oaks, Salado, (817) 947-5999. **The Inn at Salado Bed & Breakfast,** at Main Street and Pace Park, Salado, (817) 947-8200. **Mill Creek Guest Houses** (at Country Club), just off of I-35, Salado, (817) 947-5141. **Country Place Bed & Breakfast,** Route 1 Box 19VA, Salado, (817) 947-9683.

CAMPING: Stillhouse Hollow Lake (8 miles southwest of Belton), Belton, (817) 939-1829. **Belton KOA Campground** (south of Belton on I-35), Belton, (817) 939-1961. **Belton Lake Camping** (junction of FM 2271 and FM 439), Belton, (817) 939-1829.

FOR MORE INFORMATION: Salado Chamber of Commerce, P.O. Box 81, Salado, Texas, 76571, (817) 947-5040.

LOCAL BIKE SHOPS: Bicycle Outlet, 300 East Highway Business 190, Killeen, (817) 526-4209. **Killeen Bicycle Center,** 3506 East Rancier, Killeen, (817) 699-3155. **The Bike Shop,** 1141 West Rancier, Killeen, (817) 526-8054.

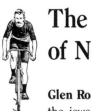

The Jewel
of North Texas Tour

Glen Rose, just 60 miles southwest of Fort Worth, is one of the jewels of North Texas. This peaceful little town is the county seat of Somervell County, which is the second smallest county in Texas and an anomaly in a state where several of the western counties are much larger than some countries. With a population of just more than 5,000 for the entire county, you will be treated to quiet roads and a very quaint little town with some especially memorable attractions.

Try to name another town Glen Rose's size where you can walk a quiet town square; go less than a block to swim in the limestone-bottomed, aqua blue **Paluxy River;** enjoy some of the best barbecue in Texas, **Hammond's** or **Maurice Pylant's Western Kitchen** (where the sauce comes in gravy boats, the sliced beef drapes over the platters' edges, and it is all topped with a big ol' slice of onion), or unforgettable Mexican and homestyle/chicken-fried specialties at **Linda's** (all on Highway 67); go on a safari in veldt-style tents with air conditioning at the **Foothills Safari Camp** (817-897-3398) at **Fossil Rim Wildlife Park;** or drive through Fossil Rim (817-897-3147) to see one of the most successful exotic wildlife preservation parks featuring cheetahs, zebras, antelope, ostriches, giraffes, rhinos, wildebeasts, and much more.

How about horseback riding in the cedar-adorned **Lake Highlands** at **The Overlook Stables** at Fossil Rim, a petting zoo and snack bar with an overlook deck and gift shop that can be accessed free

- **Starting point:** Glen Rose (loop)
- **Mileage:** 73 miles (for longest route, with shorter options ranging from 26 miles to 66 miles)
- **Terrain:** very hilly
- **Best time to ride:** September through May
- **Traffic conditions:** very light
- **Road conditions:** Good, but watch for blind corners, cattle grates, and loose gravel.

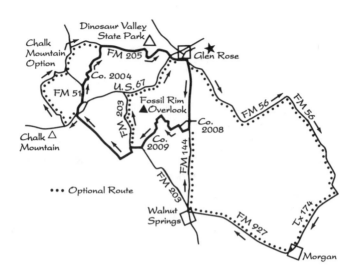

at the same overlook? Or you could catch a contemporary Christian play about the life of Christ at the **Texas Amphitheatre,** an outdoor theatre with a river running through it. Then you could put your foot in real, recognizable dinosaur prints which are preserved in the shallows of the Paluxy River at **Dinosaur Valley State Park.** The park also features miles of multileveled hiking trails with primitive sites or deluxe campsites all under the watchful eye of full-size dinosaur replicas of brontosaurus and a tyrannosaurus rex. You may also want to enjoy one of the several fantastic bed and breakfasts in the area, including the priceless **Inn on the River** with its mineral water swimming pool and wooden adirondack chairs perched on the riverbank just waiting for you and a mint julep.

Even with all these options, Glen Rose and its surrounding areas still have more to offer. Try a chuckwagon supper served by cowboys while you enjoy a western music stage show at **Tres Rios Ranch and Campground,** or visit nearby **Comanche Peak nuclear plant** where they will give you "safe" uranium power pellets (gulp!) as souvenirs. You'll also have a chance to view the controversial newly forming lake, created by the damming of the Paluxy River in the northeast part of the county, and to stay at the lodge at Fossil Rim, the former home of the wildlife park's owners, which is now an elegant bed and breakfast. I'm not making this up—you will just have to explore for yourself and soak it all in.

By the way, this is all wrapped up in a countryside covered with evergreen cedar breaks and oaks and rolling hills that offers some of the best scenery in Texas north of the Hill Country.

When you get a look at the landscape around Glen Rose, you'll believe the story of how the town got its name. Mrs. T.C. Jordan, one of the owners of **Barnard's Mill,** a grist mill on the river that is now a private residence and art museum, drew her inspiration from a vernal pastureland, much like a glen, that had roses growing naturally in it. The name is only fitting. It's like a slice of Scotland's raw and rough beauty dropped into the distinctive Texas countryside.

To begin the Glen Rose day ride, leave the charming downtown square in Glen Rose and the fantastic bakery right there. There are also freestanding public bathrooms on the courthouse square. Head south on the shoulder of FM 144.

For the short route, head 6 miles down FM 144 to County Road 2008 and turn right. For the first longer distance option of 39 additional miles, veer left on FM 56 about one-half mile from the square. Then take the following route: Stay on FM 56 at the junction with FM 202 (you will veer left), continue on FM 56 to the T intersection with TX 174 and take a right. Continue on TX 174 to **Morgan Mill,** where there are stores and food is available. Take FM 927 to the right (north) toward **Walnut Springs,** where there are more stores, and then turn right on FM 144 to return to the main route. Watch for County Road 2008 about halfway back to Glen Rose and turn left to resume the original tour if you want to continue. Follow the right angle turns of County Road 2008 for 3 miles to County Road 2009 where you turn left. This begins a very steep hill with a view that is worth every bit of the grind. At the top, on the right, is the entrance to Fossil Rim Wildlife Park's overlook.

The overlook, on the lofty rim high over the valley, does not go down into the wildlife drive tour but features a petting zoo, gift shop, overlook balcony, bathrooms, and snack bar (which serves some good food and recommendable cookies). In terms of out-in-the-country rest stops, this is paradise. You can sit out in the sun on a deck and watch giraffes and zebras frolic in the canyon below—all for no entrance fee. Be sure to load up on water and food when you leave the overlook because there are very few stores along the rest of the route. There is also very little traffic or anything else to despoil the rolling hills and scrub cedar-filled scenery.

Back at County Road 2009, turn right and go 3 miles to FM 203, at 12.0 miles total, and turn right. For the shortest route, continue on FM 203 and take a right on Highway 67 to ride 13 miles back to Glen Rose. That would be a route total of 26 miles. If you did the optional extra miles at the beginning, you would finish with 66 miles—an accomplishment in these hills.

If you are hungry for more, or did not decide to ride the optional extra miles at the beginning, turn right on FM 203 from County Road 2009 and go to the first left a couple of miles down FM 203. Turn right on this county road, which will turn left and then right to continue on to a T intersection with another county road. Turn right here and follow it 8 miles to Highway 67. You can take a right on Highway 67 and follow it right back for 11 miles for a total of 34 miles. If you like climbing, go left up Highway 67 to the top of the Chalk Mountain grade. It's about 2 miles up and has one of the best views in North Texas from the road and the roadside park, just past the top. You can go back down or take the county road to the right (northeast) at the top and wind your way down to FM 51. Just take a left on FM 51 and then a right on FM 205 and you are back on the route when you pass the Flying P County Road, entering on your right. This would add about 6 miles and incorporates the best of the route from the Chalk Mountain Metric Century, which is held in the fall.

There are some stores occasionally on Highway 67 on the way back in but they have come and gone through the years, with most lasting less than a year. It would not be prudent to count on these stores being there.

For even more miles, and one of the best routes after the back entrance to the Fossil Rim overlook, cross over Highway 67, veering right. Follow this unnumbered road until it comes upon FM 51. Take FM 51 to the left and follow it a mile or so, at 26 miles, looking for County Road 1004 which veers off to the right of a left-hand curve. Take this county road, known as Flying "P" Ranch Road, for 4 miles to FM 205 at 29.5 miles total. Go right on FM 205 for 4 miles to the entrance to Dinosaur Valley State Park. Halfway there you will encounter a significant climb of about a mile.

Either go in Dinosaur Valley State Park or come back to it later. It is one of the most memorable places in the state park annals of Texas. The hiking trails are fantastic and the camping is fine. The dinosaur tracks and the entrance, through the flat valley to the bowl ringed by hills, transport you back to prehistoric times even before you see the concrete dinosaur replicas.

To complete the ride, continue 2.8 miles more to Highway 67, cross Paluxy Road, and follow the old road into downtown. It takes you past **Barnard's Mill** on the Paluxy River.

For the entire route, without the optional extra distance in the beginning and bypassing Dinosaur Valley State Park, you're in for 36.5 miles. (If you include the optional extra miles early in the tour, the total is about 73 miles.) Either way, these are some of the best viewing and riding miles in the Lone Star State.

ACCOMMODATIONS: Inn on the River Bed and Breakfast, 209 Southwest Barnard Street, Glen Rose, (817) 897-2101. **Ye Olde Maple Inn,** 1509 Van Zandt, Glen Rose, (817) 897-3456. **Lodge at Fossil Rim,** off of Highway 67 (3 miles south of Glen Rose), Glen Rose, (817) 897-3147. **Glen Rose Motor Inn,** 300 South Big Bend Trail, Glen Rose, (817) 897-2040.

CAMPING: Dinosaur Valley State Park (5 miles west of Glen Rose), Glen Rose, (817) 897-4588. **Cedar Ridge Park** (4.5 miles south of Highway 67), Glen Rose, (817) 897-3410. **Oakdale Park,** on Highway 144 in town, Glen Rose, (817) 897-2321. **Oakdale's Camp 'n' Fish,** FM 200 to County Road 304 (4 miles east of Glen Rose, on the Brazos River), (817) 897-2478. **Keller Campground,** on FM 199, (north of town on the Brazos River), (817) 897-4003.

FOR MORE INFORMATION: Glen Rose Chamber of Commerce, P.O. Box 605, Glen Rose, Texas, 76043, (817) 897-2286.

· ·

The Best of North Texas Tour

Of all of the North Texas tours in this book, this one is for the history buff, hardcore tourist, and wayfaring wanderer who likes to explore the nooks and crannies of time and space. In other words, it's the cyclist's perfect tour. There are no theme parks, trendy shops, or touristy attractions on this tour. What is there to see? How about: part of the line of Texas frontier forts that advanced "civilization" while ensuring the end of a way of life as free and fierce as the plains wind; three of the most magnificent parks in the Texas Parks and Wildlife system; wild, wide-open spaces with empty roads that ribbon into the heart of the vistas right before your wheels; and Rockwell-esque communities with a Texas flair.

A true crossroads of time, this is where the **Goodnight-Loving Cattledrive Trail,** the **Butterfield-Overland Stage Route,** and Texas Department of Transportation's **Forts Trail** all converge. As you wander through a forest of historical markers it will seem as if you are riding in an age of crankstart tin lizzy pick-up trucks at the edge of a world transformed by the oil boom, or even in a time when wood-spoked wheels carried people much like yourself into a land of fear, uncertainty, and too much promise to turn back.

DAY ONE: Lake Mineral Wells to Jacksboro

This ride starts in **Mineral Wells.** You could spend your first night in **Weatherford,** a very nice town in its own right, which is less than 20 miles east of Mineral Wells. They have a huge first-Monday-flea market, a farmer's market just off the square where you can get plenty of those famous Parker County peaches when they are in season, and lots of good restaurants and motels, especially the newly opened Victorian House Bed and Breakfast (817) 599-9600 at the western edge of town). Call the Chamber of Commerce for more information. This could also be a good overnight stop on the way back.

- **Starting point:** Mineral Wells (loop)
- **Route:** day one—Lake Mineral Wells State Park to Jacksboro
  day two—Jacksboro to Graham
  day three—Graham to Possum Kingdom State Park
  day three (optional)—Graham to Mineral Wells
  day four—Possum Kingdom State Park to Mineral Wells
- **Mileage:** day one—43 miles (with options for 77 miles)
  day two—27 miles (with options for 47 and 50 miles)
  day three—32 miles
  day three (optional)—43 miles (with option for 47 miles)
  day four—44 miles (with option for 86 miles)
  total—146 miles (more with options)
- **Terrain:** mostly flat with several climbs
- **Best time to ride:** March through May and September through November
- **Traffic conditions:** no traffic
- **Road conditions:** excellent

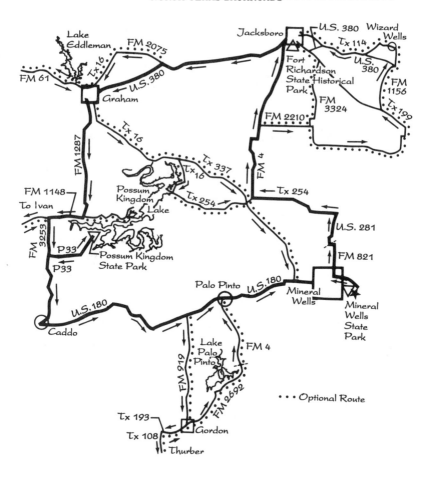

The mileage and the route description, no matter where you lodge in Mineral Wells, start at the **Lake Mineral Wells State Park.** The 90-site park is 4 miles east of the center of town on Highway 180. It is famous for its lake, the fishing, the rock climbing, and the mountain bike, equestrian, and hiking trails. It's truly a multiuse facility in a time-less setting.

Coming into town, going down the hill looking west into Min-eral Wells, are two riveting sights. The cliffs to the north of town and the plains to the left give the impression that the town is cradled in the hills, ready to slide onto the plains to the south. The other eyecatcher is the towering **Baker Hotel** in the middle of town. The Baker and its one-time competitor, the **Crazy Water Hotel,** are no longer the tourist-drawing queens of the city. The former is closed and the latter is now a retirement home. Still the glory of the grand old hotels is clearly evident—their style harkens back to the '20s, when the hotels were opened in the furor caused by the discovery of the mineral springs which some claimed could heal a laundry list of ailments. Discovered in 1881, there were more than 400 wells pumping out of those mineral springs by the 1920s.

The regal Baker Hotel, built at what was then the enormous cost of 1.2 million dollars, looms over the center of the city with architectural details that will give you a "crick" in your neck before you take them all in. Ride into town for eats, to see the hotel and all of the signs and businesses that share the label of "crazy" because of the crazy water that put the town on the map.

If you're looking for food, consider Mexican at **Pulido's** with authentic Tex-Mex, steaks and salad wagon at **K-Bob's,** home cooking at **Sarah's,** or the burgers at none other than **Chateau de Bubba's** (on the west side of town near the city park). There is also a **VF Factory Outlet** mall on the east side of town for those born to shop.

Leaving the state park, turn right on Highway 180 (Hubbard Street in town). After 1 mile you will pass **Woody's,** a Quonset burger joint teeming with atmosphere on the right. At FM 1821, 2.3 miles later, go right. In 2 more miles you will pass a cemetery with an historical marker telling you the story of Sam Savage. It will envoke a drama about the epic conflicts fought in a million small but fierce battles.

Go 3.4 miles and then turn right on Highway 281 North, where you will begin to climb the first major hill of the tour. It's not that steep or that long, but it's taxing enough. There are stores at the top if you need a break. At Highway 254, go left; there are also stores here. At 15.1 miles continue straight on Highway 254, but a 3-mile round trip to **Oran** will take you through the small community and the mother lode of historical markers that tell the story of the Goodnight-Loving trail. (Oliver Loving, whose body was carted home by his friend Charlie Goodnight after being killed by Indians, was the inspiration for the trek of Captain Call, who carried Gus McCrae in *Lonesome Dove*.) This was the site of the Black Springs Ranch, one of Goodnight's earlier ranches before he headed north. Like the trail and his fictional progeny, it's worth the trip.

Back on FM 254, continue on to **Graford,** which is 20 miles into the trip, but not before stopping 1.4 miles down the road on the return from Oran to read more historical markers on the left. In Graford, there is an authentic market, **Morrow Grocery,** the **Peppermill Square** restaurant, and more historical markers to read before leaving the bucolic little town. It might have only one major crossroads, but there is history at every turn. Take FM 4 right (north) for a long haul through some fantastic country with no stores or towns along the way to **Jacksboro.** You are truly riding into the great wide open.

Three miles out of town is an historical marker that explains some of the history of the **Kecchi Valley,** which envelops you as you pedal along. The surrounding plains and hills show little change since nineteenth-century wanderers followed the hard-packed parallel lines beneath your tour pavement.

If you are looking for more mileage, you can add 34 miles by taking FM 2210 which will be on your right at the 30-mile point in the day's ride. The longest alternative route is: Take FM 2210 to **Perrin** (where there are stores) and on through to Highway 199; ride the shoulder to FM 1156 past U.S. 380/Highway 114 to **Wizard Wells** (a nice little town); go through town, veering right on FM 1156 back to U.S. 380/Highway 114, then veer right onto County Road 920 or follow U.S. 380/Highway 114 all the way back to Highway 199, which will take you into Jacksboro. It's a heady first day's ride of 43 miles (without the longer option) for the experienced tourist but they are premium miles. There are quite a bit of climbing rollers out of Wizard Wells. This is a regular ride of the Possum Pedalers bike club of Graham (to get in touch with them, call 817-549-6127 or 817-549-3918). Check the map for shorter options, but you can't go wrong because all the roads are either quiet or have good shoulders.

Back on the main route, continue past the turnoff for FM 2210; it will be 10.6 more miles to Highway 380. There you go right on Highway 380 and head into Jacksboro. You will pass the **Chuck Wagon Café** on the way in for home cooking. At 42.6 total miles you will hit the town square. The Chamber of Commerce is not hard to find just off the southeast corner of the square. Go right on Highway 199 about 2 miles to get to the **Fort Richardson State Historical Park.**

In town you can easily find most of the motels. All of the accommodations are either northwest or southeast of the square on Highway 199. There is the **Green Frog Restaurant** for steaks, salads, and such. On the way out to the park is **Dairyland BBQ** which features all sorts of home cooking, barbecue, fish, Tex-Mex, and just about anything edible. They also serve huge schooners of good ol' ice tea.

Fort Richardson State Historical Park, with 23 campsites, is a relatively quiet park in spite of the wealth of military history, buildings, and parade ground that almost echo with bugles as you soak it all in. It has an 8-acre quarry lake, hiking trails, and some great campsites. It is a short trip to and from Jacksboro, unusually close to the city for a Texas state park. The fort is about one-fourth the size of the town it spawned when it was established in 1866. Even though the fort only lasted 12 years, it played an important part in the conflict between the chain of frontier forts, of which Fort Richardson was the northernmost. It was the place where General William T. Sherman was headed when he narrowly missed an Indian ambush in 1871. A wagon train of teamsters the next day was not so lucky. The general, who had been recalcitrant until that time, reacted by appointing Colonel Ranald S. Mackenzie to retaliate. This was the first in a series of events that would eventually drive the various warring tribes out of Texas or into submission in less than 7 more years.

This is just the beginning of the history of the nine remaining buildings, which include the elegant wooden officers' quarters—the only of their kind in the country still standing.

DAY TWO: Jacksboro to Graham

This is the easiest day with only a few options. The route basically follows the shoulder and wide lanes of Highway 380 for 27 miles into **Graham.** This is mainly because the trip out of the western side of Graham to **Fort Belknap** and back is a wonderful little jaunt of 20 miles. You could do this in the afternoon or make another easy day of it and spend two nights in the Eisenhower-era Graham.

Leave Jacksboro by turning left off the square on well-marked Highway 380, follow it 12.9 miles to **Bryson,** and then on the remaining 13.7 miles into Graham. An alternative route is to veer right on FM 2075 just out of Bryson to Highway 16, and go left (south) into Graham. This adds only 3 miles to the trip and gets you off the major road for awhile. Upon entering Graham on Highway 16 continue south (also Elm Street). Highway 380 will take you straight into town as well. The bike shop, and the refurbished movie theater, The National, are located on the square, as well as a host of other businesses. In the middle of the town square is the oak tree where the Southwestern Cattlemen's Association was formed. Continue on Highway 16 South (Elm Street) to see the shady town avenue and to get to most of the local restaurants—try **Sanderson's BBQ** (which has steaks, home cooking, and a buffet). You will retrace this route out of the center of town to depart the next day. To go to Fort Belknap, instead of heading into town, go north until you hit Highway 16/67, and head out on FM 61. You will ride past picturesque **Lake Graham** which is connected to **Lake Eddleman** by a canal. Take FM 3003, to the right, 3.1 miles out of town if you want to see the lake, visit the marina, or pick up something at the stores near there.

At exactly 10 miles, just after you pass the black plastic horse on the left, you will see the walls for Fort Belknap, founded in 1851.

There are no stores at the fort, but you can get water. You can ride the 3 or so miles into **Newcastle** where there are stores if you should need them. At the fort there are several buildings, umpteen historical markers, a museum, and a picnic arbor draped with one of the largest known grapevines, which have been growing since the '30s. The parade grounds, the desolate setting, and the native stone buildings carry you right back to the fort's heydey.

Fort Belknap closed in 1859 but is extremely well preserved. Its restoration began with the Texas centennial in 1936 and ended with the addition of the archives building in 1976. There are more stories and murdered ghosts amid the fort's mist than we can tell in this space, but don't miss the chance to wander around Fort Belknap.

When you leave the fort, just retrace your route and ride the 10 miles back into friendly Graham, the host of March's Possum Pedal 100, a grand cycling event that draws 2,500 riders each spring.

DAY THREE: Graham to Possum Kingdom

Depending on your schedule decide whether to return to Mineral Wells the third day or to ride another day and go on to **Possum Kingdom, Palo Pinto,** and then back to the home of Crazy Water. There are some climbs and if there is wind, it can be strenuous. But the views of Possum Kingdom are postcard quality.

The route back to Minerals Wells, briefly described, is: Take Highway 16 south out of Graham and follow it 2.4 miles until it veers left, staying on it. This is one of the last places to grab supplies unless you go into **Pickwick** (on the shore route near the lake) or ride into Graford (less than a mile) at the intersection of Highway 337 and Highway 254. Twelve miles out, Highway 16 veers off to the right and the continuing road becomes Highway 337. To save a couple of miles, stay on Highway 337. For a more scenic and hilly route, stay on Highway 16 which runs along the eastern shore of Possum Kingdom Lake. After you've gone 17.7 miles of the shore route, you can stay on Highway 16 or FM 2335 into Pickwick for 3 to 4 extra miles. Then take Highway 16 which will become Highway 254 and follow that to the intersection with Highway 337, just east of Graford. The shore route turns right on Highway 337 while the straight route continues on. This will wind up and down a few bluffs before making a long drop toward Mineral Wells. When you T into U.S. 180, go left. On your right will be **El Paseo** Mexican restaurant. Treat yourself to an indulgent meal—you're finished for the most part. In 4 miles you will be back in the center of Mineral Wells and the park is just 2 miles beyond that. If you take the straight route back from Graham on Highway 337 and U.S. 180, it is a total of 43 miles. If you take the slightly longer shore route, without the optional jaunt into Pickwick, your total will be 47 miles.

The continuation to Possum Kingdom will appeal most to those camping because the town's accommodation choices are slim. The best place to stay is at **Possum Kingdom State Recreation Park,** which has 116 campsites and 16 cabins.

The 1,615-acre park has swimming facilities, lighted fishing pier, boats for rent, a park store, and even a herd of Texas Longhorn grazing in the open range around the entrance road. It is also a haven for scuba diving. Contact dive shops in the Fort Worth/Dallas area for details about dives in the lake that can be as deep as 150 feet!

Possum Kingdom Lake (known as "PK" to anyone in the area for more than 5 minutes) was created by the Morris Sheppard Dam, which was built by the agency that became the Brazos River Authority, one of the forces in Texas water rights control. Rumor is that Franklin D. Roosevelt, whose WPA did quite a bit of the work in forming the lake, named the body of water himself.

Leave Graham by heading south on Highway 16. After 2.4 miles, veer right on FM 1287. You are on part of the course of the Possum Pedal 100 bike ride. Continue south on FM 1287; at 3.7 miles you will cross the muddy **Brazos River** (the poetic name comes from **los brazos a los Dios,** which means the arms of God.) In another 12.2 miles, you will pass stores on the left.

Here FM 1148 goes left to cover the north shore of the lake. There are a few hills, some spectacular views, and a couple of really simple but exquisite restaurants down this road. Of note is **Possum Hollow** about 5 miles in. They make a broiled lemon catfish that has boaters cruising all the way across the lake to savor it.

By the way, if you are looking for driving side trips, try **South Bend** where the **Stovall Hot Wells** feature sulfurous mineral springs that promise to "boil out the poison." South Bend is on Highway 67 about 10 miles southwest of Graham.

If you don't follow the north shore, go right at the T that makes FM 1287 become FM 1148. Go 4.7 more miles to FM 3253 and head south by turning left. You will just have climbed "Bertha," a hill of note on the Possum Pedal 100 course.

If you want to get some lunch, stay on FM 1148 and you will ride into **Ivan** in 5 miles. There is a store and **Daddy D's Damn Good Barbeque.** It is damn good—try anything on the menu.

Back on FM 3253, go south 5 miles and turn left on P33, the road that leads into the park 6 miles later. You will enter the park at the headquarters and can roam all over the place once you're inside and settled. Again, there is a park store but Ivan is the nearest town.

DAY FOUR: Possum Kingdom State Park to Mineral Wells

Leaving the park that day or the next morning, you retrace your steps back out P33 to FM 3253, staying on P33 by going left. You will ride 8.5 more miles to get to **Caddo,** where there is little else but **Caddo Mercantile**—a little if-we-don't-have-it, you-don't-need-it store on Highway 180.

The rest of the route is easy. Follow part of the Butterfield Overland Stage route along Highway 180, a rolling wide-shouldered old-fashioned highway, for 28 miles into Mineral Wells. That will give you a total of 44 miles for the day.

If you wish to be adventurous and are starved for miles, add a fantastic route by turning right (south) on FM 919 to go to **Gordon** (where there are stores), turn right on Highway 193 to **Mingus,** and go right on Highway 108 to **Thurber.** Thurber is a ghost town that once was a thriving center for brick manufacturing and coal mining. Definitely try either the **New York Hill** restaurant, with its view on the south side of I-20, or the **Smokestack** on the north side. If you don't find the hot rolls at the Smokestack to be the best you've ever had, I don't know why—I think they're almost as good as my wife's Aunt Mary's.

Backtrack to Mingus, then Gordon, and take FM 2692 to the right for some climbing and magnificent views of **Lake Palo Pinto.** (The maps don't show FM 2692 connecting to FM 4 but it does.) Hit FM 4 and go left back to Highway 180 at Palo Pinto where there are stores. Here you are only 11 miles from Mineral Wells. Leaving the lake on the way to Palo Pinto you will climb **Whit Mountain,** which is much better to go down than up—it's about a 2-mile climb and one of the longest in the area. This ride-of-a-lifetime side trip will add about 42 miles for a total of 86 miles for the day. It would be quite an accomplishment and a climbing tour de force.

Now you are back in Mineral Wells. If you wish to see more frontier forts in the area, contact the Texas Department of Transportation to get a copy of their Texas Forts Trail map or pick up one at a state line visitor's center. Other garrisons worth seeing while in the area are: **Fort Griffin** (15 miles north of Albany, just west of this tour), **Fort Phantom Hill** (north of Abilene), **Fort Chadbourne** (10 miles north of Bronte, between Abilene and San Angelo), **Fort Concho** (in San Angelo), and many others within reasonable driving distance.

Enjoy these slices of history, reminders of the bloody conflict that established a new world order in an untamed land that is still, for the most part, untamed. And you get to ride through all of this . . . enjoy.

ACCOMMODATIONS: Hillcrest Motel, 2319 S. Oak, Mineral Wells, (817) 325-2626. **Days Inn of Mineral Wells,** 3701 East Hubbard, Mineral Wells, (817) 325-6961. **Pinto Inn,** 2809 Highway 180 West, Mineral Wells, (817) 328-1111. **Skyline Motel,** 3603 Highway 180 East, Mineral Wells, (817) 325-4433. **Twelve Oaks Inn,** 4103 Highway 180 East, Mineral Wells, (817) 325-6956. **Hillcrest Motel,** 544 North Main, Jacksboro, (817) 567-5542, **Jacksboro Inn,** 704 South Main, Jacksboro, (817) 567-3751. **Gateway Inn,** 1401 Highway 16 South, Graham, (817) 549-0222. **Plantation Inn,** 1212 Highway 16 South, Graham, (817) 549-8320. **Travelers Inn,** 1516 Highway 16 South, Graham, (817) 549-0274. **Possum Kingdom Lodge** (northeast corner of the lake off of Highway 16 North), Caddo, (817) 779-2757.

CAMPING: Lake Mineral Wells State Park (3 miles east of Mineral Wells on U.S. 180), Mineral Wells (817) 328-1171. **Mitchell's RV Park** (16 miles north of Mineral Wells), Mineral Wells, (817) 328-1171. **Weatherford KOA** (junction of I-20 and Highway 51), Weatherford, (817) 594-8801. **Fort Richardson State Historical Park** (southwest edge of city), Jacksboro, (817) 567-3506. **Lakeshore Marina & RV Park** (east end of FM 1148), Graham, 1-800-542-4361. **Fireman's Park** (on Highway 67 toward Breckenridge), Graham, (817) 549-3324. **Kindley Park** (6 miles out of Graham on Highway 380), Graham, (817) 549-3324. **Lake Eddelman** (1 mile out of town on U.S. 380 North), Graham, (817) 549-3324. **Possum Kingdom State Recreation Area** (18 miles north of Caddo on Park Road 33), Caddo, (817) 549-1803. **Rock Creek Camp** (17 miles south of Graham on Highway 16), Caddo, (817) 779-2766.

FOR MORE INFORMATION: Mineral Wells Chamber of Commerce, Mineral Wells, Texas, 76067, 1-800-252-MWTX. **Jacksboro Chamber of Commerce,** 102 South Main Street, Jacksboro, Texas, 76458, (817) 567-2602, **Graham Chamber of Commerce,** 608 Elm Street, Graham, Texas, 76450, (817) 549-3355.

LOCAL BIKE SHOPS: Mike's Bike Shop, 721 East Street, Graham, (817) 549-6322.

Northeast Texas Pineywoods Tour

This multiday, multioption tour will give you the best of East Texas. It is designed to introduce you to the lakes, quaint towns, people, and flora and fauna of the region. You will cover every type of vegetative life form Northeast Texas offers, including the Bassboat Bubba. Warning: This particular creature can be a nasty companion on the roads near any of the lakes, particularly on the weekends. So be careful and use your rearview mirror and whistle, which I heartily recommend you carry on any tour.

This is a combination of day trip loops and place-to-place touring. Any of it can be stretched by going on to the next town and riding back in the same day. In that respect, except for the Jefferson to Longview segment, you can do it all from Tyler.

Tyler, a bustling town of 75,000 plus, is the rose capital of the world. If you've ever seen the city during the Azalea Festival the first

- **Starting point:** Tyler (loop)
- **Route:** day one—Tyler area loop
  day two—Tyler to Gladewater
  day three—Gladewater to Pittsburg
  day four—Pittsburg to Jefferson
  day five—Jefferson to Longview
  day six—Longview to Tyler
- **Mileage:** day one—36 miles (or more with options)
  day two—33 miles (or more with options)
  day three—43 miles
  day four—49 miles
  day five—39 miles (or 50 miles with option)
  day six—50 miles (or only 36 with option)
  total—250 miles
- **Terrain:** mostly flat with rolling hills interspersed throughout
- **Best time to ride:** September through May
- **Traffic conditions:** heavy near towns, nonexistent on rural roads
- **Road conditions:** good, busy roads have wide shoulders

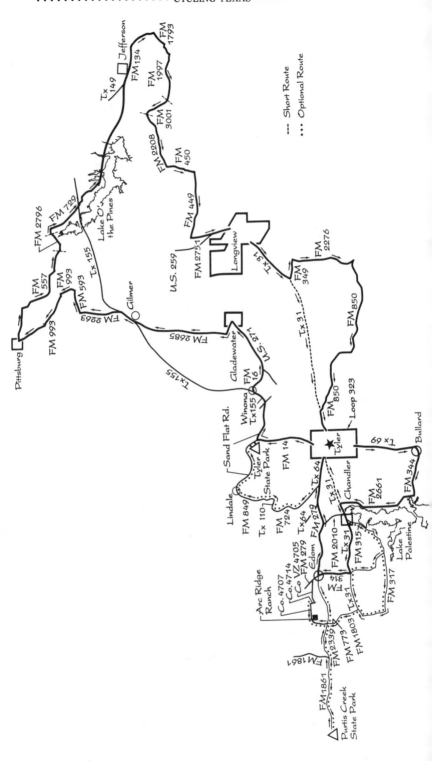

week in April, you might think it is the capital of all flowers, including the lush, florid azalea bushes that explode that week. It is also the home of the Tyler Bike Club (TBC), a rapid-riding, friendly bike club that hosts two or three regular rides a week (one is in this book) but none on Sunday morning.

Tyler, through East Texas Rails to Trails (ETRTT), will soon be the home of the first major railroad converted to a biking/hiking/ equestrian trail in the state of Texas. It will run from south of Tyler in **Bullard** to near Jacksonville, ending near **Love's Lookout.** It will be 19 miles each way through some of the most beautiful forested country, cleaved as only a quiet railroad right of way could. Maps will be available in town as soon as construction is completed (it started mid-1992); call ETRTT at (903) 566-6907 for information. That's one more option where it's finished.

A day-one option would be to ride from Tyler on the Saturday Bullard ride with the Tyler Bike Club. They meet every Saturday morning, ride to Bullard (usually) for pancakes and then on to various mileages. Read on for directions that will guide you along much of their route if you want to ride to another town or if you are not starting on Saturday and cannot join the TBC crew.

The other days will lead you to **Arc Ridge Guest Ranch** or **Gladewater,** or you can return to Tyler to ride or drive to Gladewater for day two's trek. Then it's Gladewater to **Pittsburg,** and Pittsburg to Jefferson or Longview. If you go to Longview, you can return to Tyler the same day or do the Longview to Jefferson weekender two-day ride. Or you can go directly to Jefferson and then on into Longview and Tyler because the Longview-Jefferson route doubles back a lot and you will still see most of the great route between these two cities.

Here we go, including digressions on the various options. Get out a pencil and paper to keep up with the options, then total up your choice. Here is a juicy tour through the Northeast Texas Pineywoods, starting with Tyler.

DAY ONE: Tyler and Environs Loop

Head out with Tyler Bike Club or on your own down Highway 69 on the shoulder. It is busy, but it's flat and a good shoulder. Don't worry—it gets much better.

Turn right on FM 344 into Bullard, the future home of the northern terminus of the Rail-to-Trail conversion. You can see the park-like right-of-way right there in the middle of town. **Sherry's,** on the right up FM 2493 a block or two, is the breakfast spot with the pancakes to prove it.

Stay on FM 344 through **Teaselville** and on to the eastern shore of **Lake Palestine.** It bends right (north) and you should continue on until you cross Highway 155, where FM 344 becomes FM 2661. Continue on to Highway 31 (when you pass FM 2813, you could turn right and go about 3 miles into **Noonday** where the sweetest onions in Texas are grown and sold), where you will get on a wide shoulder and ride into **Chandler,** where there are stores and restaurants. Here you leave the Tyler club route and trace part of Tyler's Beauty & the Beast tour, the Tour of the Little Apple (put on by the TBC), and the route from Arc Ridge Guest Ranch. At this point you have 35 miles under your belt.

This is a major option location. You can return to Tyler on the Highway 31 shoulder (11 miles to Loop 323) for a short day trip (36 miles total), if the club has not already led you south for a long ride. Or you can take a long route around to Arc Ridge Guest Ranch, which will be described in detail later, or go directly there through **Edom** by connecting with FM 2010 out of Chandler and then turning left on FM 279 (20 miles to the ranch—details on route from Edom to the ranch follow—for a 55-mile day total).

Edom, an artsy-craftsy community, has a very good lunch and dinner joint called **The Shed,** located at the crossroads in the little town. There is also the **Red Rooster Bed and Breakfast** as well as a couple of other bed and breakfasts in the area, for planned or emergency accommodations.

If you are doing a route out of Arc Ridge Guest Ranch, you will loop through Edom. If you are not going to the ranch, you can head for camping by going to **Tyler State Park** or **Purtis Creek State Recreation Area.** It is 38 miles to Tyler State Park from Edom via 279 to Highway 64. Take a left on FM 724, a right on Highway 110, and a left on FM 849 to **Lindale.** Head out of Lindale on Jim Hogg Road—named after the first native-born Governor of Texas, who had a daughter named Ima (I don't make up this stuff)—and turn left on Sandy Flat Road to Highway 14. Turn right on Highway 14 and follow it down to the park entrance. It is a 17-mile trip each way to **Purtis Creek** from Edom. Take FM 2339 to FM 1861, turn left, and continue on FM 1861 to the park. There is a store at 8.6 miles from Edom near the park entrance. Both routes will require that you return to Tyler or pick up day two's route on the overall tour.

Arc Ridge Guest Ranch is a bicycling-friendly place, largely because its owner, Charlie Ogilvie, is a very friendly bicyclist. His energy and high-voltage smile are contagious. A veteran tourist, Ogilvie also does marathons and triathlons, even though he is seventy-something. Charlie and his gracious wife Reva offer bed & breakfast comfort in two cottages. They also have group facilities, screened shelters with electricity and showers, camping areas, hiking trails, a lake, fishing facilities, and a bike repair and storage area.

The lake is a controlled habitat for Charlie's experiment with alligators and other wildlife. He is also building a shrine/meditation shelter dedicated to American Indians on one of the many developed hiking trails on the 600-acre ranch. These are two of the most unique and special people in Texas—you really should meet them. Stay at the ranch or ride from here if you can. It is a biking Xanadu.

Back at Chandler, to do the rest of the route, drop by or stay at the ranch and return to Tyler to end day one. Follow Highway 31 to FM 1803 for a shorter route, or for a longer route, take County Road 315 out of Chandler. Turn right on County Road 317 and pass County Road 314. (Turn right on County Road 314 to go to **Brownsboro** and on to Edom for another shortcut. The ranch will be out 279 to County Road VZ 4705. Turn right on County Road 4714 and left on County Road 4707 to get to the ranch, which is about 7 miles from Edom.) Turn right on FM 1803 16 miles from Chandler, continue on FM 1803 4 miles to Highway 31, and go right 1 mile and left on FM 1803 again. You will hit County Road 773 in 5 miles and turn right onto it, cross FM 2339, and go 4.5 more miles to County Road VZ 4707. Turn right on VZ 4707 and follow it a couple of miles to the ranch's entrance. There's a sign, so you can't miss it.

To return to Tyler, backtrack, continue, or leave the ranch and head to Edom, take 279 to Highway 64 and ride its shoulder back into Tyler. The total mileage for the ride to Bullard, to Chandler, the long way to the ranch, to Edom, and back to Tyler is roughly 80 miles for the day, measuring from Tyler's Loop 323. If you come from farther in town or take any side trips, add on the appropriate mileage.

DAY TWO: Tyler to Gladewater

Depending on whether you are now situated at Purtis Creek, Arc Ridge Guest Ranch, or Edom, make your way back to Tyler and add that mileage to the total. If leaving from Tyler, the route begins at the edge of town, so add the distance from your accommodations. If you are in Tyler State Park, subtract the distance when it is passed on the route. You are on your way to Gladewater.

This side of the Hill Country, and maybe even surpassing those locales, Gladewater is quickly evolving into antique central. There are dozens of large shops, several antique single-building mini-malls, and many of the other cute attendant businesses that spring up from such traffic—tea rooms, bed and breakfasts, shops, boutiques, and bakeries. Of particular interest is the **Busy Bee Sweet Shop** and their breads, pies, and cheesecakes, with the **Honeycomb Suites** bed and breakfast above it—a cyclist's idea of perfection if there ever was one.

To go from Tyler to Gladewater (33 miles measuring from Tyler Loop 323 to downtown Gladewater) start at Loop 323 in north Tyler and head out Highway 14, past Tyler State Park (there's a store at the entrance). At 6.5 miles, turn on a county road (also posted as Sand Flat Road) crossing County Road 14 just north of the park entrance. Turn right and stay on the road, hit Highway 155, go left into **Winona** (where there are also stores and food), take County Road 16 out of Winona to Highway 271, and stay on its shoulder. Or take the alternate road 1 mile after hitting Highway 271, where it veers to the right and parallels the highway and has no designation or sign. Stay on Highway 271 (or on the alternate road until it hits Highway 135, then go left back to Highway 271) and follow it into the heart of Gladewater. Because extra mileage may have been added for tourists who had to ride to Tyler to start, this is a short day of 33 miles. Tomorrow will be a medium day to Pittsburg.

DAY THREE: Gladewater to Pittsburg

Like day one's route, this one works as a day trip as well. It can also be shortened. Both options utilize Highway 271, a straight shot into Pittsburg of 32 miles on road with traffic but with a good shoulder all the way. To day trip, take the backroads route described and return to Gladewater on Highway 271 for a 75-mile day. Needless to say, the backroads route contains the quiet roads and spectacular scenery that will spoil you on this tour.

Leave Gladewater on Main Street (Highway 271). At .7 mile turn left on Gay Street, and pass the high school on the left at 2.3 miles. Turn right on FM 2685 at 3.2 miles. Stay on FM 2685 until you have gone 13.3 miles then turn right on Highway 155 (turn left to go to Big Sandy which has shops, bed and breakfasts, and some choice Victorian houses and is 12 miles to west). You will hit **Gilmer** and more stores at 16 miles. At 19.7 miles turn left on FM 2263, then turn right on FM 593 26 miles into the trip. Turn left on FM 993 at 33.6 miles and you will be alongside the **Bolton Cemetery.**

A tourist is tested by how many historical markers he or she stops to read. But you're truly a tourist if you explore what the marker talks about. There are usually signs on the road a mile before each marker that tell you they are coming up. I recommend that you don't miss any of them.

A perfect example is the tableau of history that unfolds when you read the Bolton Cemetery marker. It tells the story of Colonel Ebb Bolton, who died in 1877 after fighting for the Confederacy in the Civil War. After the war, he freed his slaves, many of whom stayed on and were buried in the cemetery alongside him and his wife Martha, who died in 1881. The limestone markers of the Jewish gravestones of the Boltons are right alongside many freedmen's and more recent austere graves; they were interred right inside the wrought-iron fences as equals. This is not your typical image of the Old South, but one that may be much more common than many are aware of. This is the kind of time travel that historical markers seen from the seat of a bike can create.

Exit the cemetery and return to FM 993, staying on it until you cross Highway 271 at 42.9 miles and stay on Lafayette Street as you come into Pittsburg until you hit Highway 11 (also posted as Quitman) and go left into downtown.

To stay or camp out at **Lake Bob Sandlin,** head out of town on Quitman (Highway 11) and turn right on FM 1520 (at 1.5 miles cross Loop 179). Continue on to the lake, which is about 5 miles out. There are several stores and campgrounds out there in addition to the state park.

Downtown Pittsburg is one of the cleanest, most well-kept Rockwellesque downtowns to be found anywhere. There is a prayer tower of imported European old world craftsmanship downtown where the clock, donated by Bo Pilgrim of Pilgrim's Pride (a southern poultry producer), chimes "When the Saints Go Marching In" each hour. The chicken plants and feeders in the 25-mile radius of town house as many as a half million chickens at one time. The thriving business is a great deal of what has preserved and maintained the kind atmosphere of Pittsburg. Pilgrim's enormous mansion on the outskirts of town on U.S. 271 North is affectionately known as Cluckingham Palace. This is a small town to be savored.

Eats in Pittsburg worth checking out include **Al's Place** for pizza in the center of town. Just off the main street to the left (west) when heading north on Marshall Street is **Warrick's** where the Ezekiel Airship, an early flight attempt that supposedly predates the Wright brothers' by years, took place. Next door to it is the **Pittsburg East Texas Hot Link,** a decidedly unhealthful, super hot sausage that is so good it has to be tasted to be described. Note the freshly painted Eisenhower-era signs on all of the buildings downtown. If the fictional town of Cicely, Alaska, in the television show *Northern Exposure* had a Texas twin, it would be Pittsburg. Day two ends here or you can head back down U.S. 271 to Tyler.

DAY FOUR: Pittsburg to Jefferson

From here you can return to Gladewater by U.S. 271 (32 miles) and back to Tyler on U.S. 271, which turns into Highway 175 (27 more miles to the Tyler loop) in a long day or two short days. To return from Pittsburg directly to Longview to finish the route instead of going back to Gladewater, retrace U.S. 271 to Gilmer, follow it out of Gilmer, then take FM 300 just at the south side of town to the left (southeast). Follow FM 300 all the way into Longview (40 miles to the center of Longview). Or you can take the following route to Jefferson: Use the overnight information in the Longview-Jefferson weekender tour, and return by the second day's route.

To get from Pittsburg to Jefferson, head out of town on FM 557, take it for 18 miles to FM 2796, and go left on FM 2796. Follow FM 2796 to **Lone Star** at the tip of Lake O' the Pines and turn right in town on FM 729. Follow FM 729 for 23 miles until it hits Highway 49 just 4 miles out of Jefferson. (Note: At the intersection with FM 726, you can go right and ride just a couple of miles to see the Lake O' the Pines spillway, as described in the Longview-Jefferson weekender—it's worth the trip.) FM 729 makes up most of this route and is busy on weekends. Leave early if you plan to be on it those days. Otherwise, it is a beautiful road that crosses the lake's estuaries a half dozen times. There are stores in Lone Star and near the lake.

In Jefferson, cross Highway 59, staying on Highway 49 (also posted as Broadway) until you get to Polk Street, turn right, and head for downtown. See the Longview-Jefferson weekender for details on what to see and do in Jefferson.

DAY FIVE: Jefferson to Longview

Follow the Jefferson to Longview route detailed in the Longview-Jefferson weekender (see page 104). You can do day two's route or reverse day one's route (Day one is shorter, at 39.2 miles, versus 49.6 miles, and prettier).

DAY SIX: Longview to Tyler

This route is admittedly not that interesting, but its sole purpose is to get you back to Tyler. It is borrowed, with a few changes, from the Texas Chainring Challenge '92. Head out of town on Highway 31 to **Kilgore** to FM 349, which is about 15 miles depending on where you start in Longview. Turn left on FM 349 and ride to FM 2276 (there's a store here). Take FM 2276 to FM 850 and go right, cross Highway 259 (there are more stores here), and continue on FM 850 through **New London** and **Overton** (both have stores and food). Continue on FM 850 all the way into Tyler (you may also take a left on Highway 31 and follow it into town).

You will hit Loop 323 in Tyler on the east side at one of the few quiet locales. From there you will have to find your way to your car or accommodations. Total distance from center of Longview to Tyler Loop 323: 50 miles. You can take the straight and narrow and stay on Highway 31/259 through Kilgore and follow the shoulder on Highway 31 straight into Tyler and shorten the trip by 36 miles. It's busy but there's a shoulder all the way.

In spite of the confusion so many options can cause, this is a good tour no matter what length you do. This basically covers the great spots in Northeast Texas, but only a small portion of what it offers. You'll come back soon—the pines will be calling.

ACCOMMODATIONS: Best Western Inn, 2828 Northwest Loop 323, Tyler, (903) 595-2681. **Rosevine Inn Bed & Breakfast,** 415 South Vine, Tyler, (903) 592-2221. **Mary's Attic Bed & Breakfast,** 417 South College, Tyler, (903) 592-5181. **Arc Ridge Guest Ranch** (bed and breakfast and camping), P.O. Box 7 (5 miles south of town off of FM 773 and County Road 4707), Ben Wheeler, (903) 833-5337, **Wild Briar Inn Bed and Breakfast,** Box 2175754, Ben Wheeler, (903) 852-3975. **La Villa Gardens,** 205 North Greer, Pittsburg, (903) 856-6574. **Texas Street Bed and Breakfast,** 218 North Texas Street, Pittsburg, (903) 856-7552. **Carson House,** 302 Mount Pleasant Street, Pittsburg, (903) 856-2468. See the Longview and Jefferson Weekender tour for information on accommodations for those cities.

CAMPING: Tyler State Park (10 miles north of Tyler off of FM 14), Tyler, (903) 597-5338. **Arc Ridge Guest Ranch** (camping and bed and breakfast), P.O. Box 7 (5 miles south of town off of FM 773 and County Road 4707), Ben Wheeler, (903) 833-5337. **Bob Sandlin State Park,** (northeast of Pittsburg on FM 127 and FM 21), (903) 572-5371. **Purtis**

Creek State Park, Route 1 Box 506 (off of FM 316 North), Eustace, (903) 425-2332. **Fish Hawk Marine,** Route 1 Box 102 (off of FM 3440), Hawkins, (903) 769-2134. **Lake Holbrook Park** (4 miles northwest of Mineola off U.S. 69), Mineola, (903) 763-2716. **Monticello Park** (8 miles southwest of Mount Pleasant via FM 127), Mount Pleasant, (903) 572-3991.

FOR MORE INFORMATION: Tyler Chamber of Commerce, 407 North Broadway, Tyler, Texas, 75702, (903) 592-1661. **Pittsburg Chamber of Commerce,** 202 Jefferson Street, Pittsburg, Texas, 75686, (903) 856-3442.

LOCAL BIKE SHOPS: Bike World, 322 East Southeast Loop 323, Suite 110, Tyler, (903) 581-5002. **Simpson's Bike & Sail,** Highway 110 South, Tyler, (903) 561-4810. **Ten Speed & Sport,** 4111 Troup Highway, Tyler, (903) 597-2488.

PANHANDLE
CANYONS AND PLAINS

• • •

Rebecca Kinserlow

Come to the Texas Panhandle and explore one of the finest places to cycle anywhere. The variety of terrain can be extreme: Miles and miles of pancake-flat roads to canyons and arroyos deliver exhilarating drops and challenging climbs. Most days are favored with blue skies, bright sunshine, and gorgeous sunsets.

Early settlers to the area described it as "an ocean of land," and even with today's network of roads and interstate highways, the immensity of the land is sometimes overwhelming. Covering over 60,000 square miles is a nearly flat, treeless expanse larger than the combined states of Maryland, Massachusetts, New Hampshire, Vermont, and Connecticut. The region contains the headwaters of three major Texas rivers: the **Red,** the Colorado, and the Brazos.

The first human occupants of the area were hunters who used Clovis- and Folsom-type spear points, dating back to about 12,000 years ago. They hunted mammoth, giant bison, camel, and horse, all long extinct now. The **Lubbock Lake Site,** just off Loop 289, is a national historic landmark and a Texas State Park where you can learn more about the archaeology and geology of the area. (The park hours are 9 A. M. to 5 P.M. Tuesday through Saturday and 1 P.M. to 5 P.M. on Sunday.)

Centuries later, the nomadic Apache and Comanche tribes hunted and sheltered here. In 1541 Francisco Vasquez de Coronado was the first European to explore the area while searching futilely for the gold and riches of Quivera. The buffalo hunters, the railroaders, the cattlemen, the farmers, and the oilmen followed in the ensuing years. This is where the Old South met the Old West. This wonderful history is documented at the **Ranching Heritage Center** in Lubbock, which has more than fourteen acres of authentic nineteenth- and twentieth-century build-ings, and at the **Panhandle-Plains Museum** in Canyon, which offers pioneer history and the Don Harrington Petroleum Wing.

When looking over a map of the area, remember that it is sometimes a long way between towns and there may no longer be any people in the town named on your map. Before touring secondary roads without motorized support, please check on the availability of water with local residents.

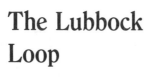

The Lubbock Loop

This 49-mile loop will take you through canyons and flat to gently rolling terrain in Lubbock County. It should be challenging and enjoyable for recreational cyclists of any ability. You will be seeing the agricultural industries of the area as well as learning about the history and prehistory of **Lubbock** and the surrounding South Plains. Early spring and late fall are excellent times to see migrating birds; spring and early summer bring abundant wildflowers and butterflies; summer through fall is the growing and harvesting season; and even during the winter, when the landscape is a dramatic, stark contrast to the verdant lushness of summer, many days are warm enough for a ride.

Because this is a loop ride, you can begin and end anywhere along the route. If you're camping you will enjoy **Buffalo Springs Lake,** which is also a good place to start. If you're driving through the area, begin in **Slaton** (12 miles east of Lubbock on U.S. Highway 84) from **George's Fina Station and Café** on the Highway 84 access road.

From Buffalo Springs Lake: As you leave the park, turn south onto FM 835. You'll travel through your first canyon with a short but rather steep climb. Immediately after cresting the canyon, turn right onto FM 3020 for the next 2.7 miles. To the north, you'll see a large prairie dog town. These small mammals are fascinating to watch and can be real clowns. (Don't pick them up or play with them because they harbor fleas and ticks which can transmit diseases to humans.)

You may catch the scent of the **Lubbock Feed Lots** before you see them. This operation brings in calves weighing about 600

- **Starting point:** Lubbock (loop)
- **Mileage:** 49 miles
- **Terrain:** rolling to steep climbs
- **Best time to ride:** good year-round
- **Traffic conditions:** light
- **Road conditions:** good

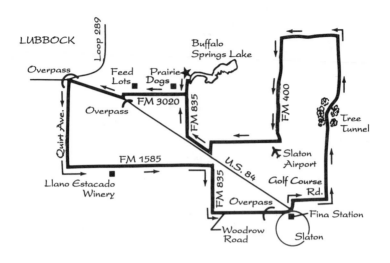

pounds, feeds them for 5 months and ships the finished cattle to pack-ers who then sell the beef to restaurants and supermarkets. Annually, they finish and ship one hundred ten thousand head of cattle. You'll likely see horse-mounted cowboys in the pens, a reminder of how close this world is to the Old West. After you pass the cattle pens and cross the railroad tracks, continue directly across Spur 331 and curve onto Highway 84 for 2.6 miles.

You will be turning left (south) from the highway at the first signal (before the overpass) onto Quirt Avenue. Usually the traffic is light but this is a narrow road, so be cautious here. You will ride south for 3.7 miles. On the left you will see **Town and Country Airport.** Depending on the season, there will be many small planes used for crop dusting darting in and out of the fields.

When you intersect with FM 1585, turn left (east). This is an excellent biking road with wide shoulders and light traffic. You will see fields of sunflowers, cotton, and soybeans stretching away on either side of the road. Just ahead on the right, is **Llano Estacado Winery.** The warm days and cool nights here produce excellent wine grapes and Llano Estacado wines have won awards worldwide. Stop for a tour of the facilities and a complimentary wine tasting.

After touring the winery, continue east on FM 1585 for 5 miles to FM 835 and turn right (south); continue for 2 miles. Turn left (east) on Woodrow Road and ride 2.7 miles into Slaton. This small commu-nity was built as the terminus for the Santa Fe Railroad in 1910 after railroad officials and Lubbock civic leaders were unable to compromise on a site in Lubbock. It is still a vital rail center for the area. Just after you ride under the overpass, you'll see George's Fina Station and Café on your right. Stop here for the best cheese rolls ever—yeasty, crusty, and full of melted cheddar cheese—and be sure your water bottles are full before you leave.

When you leave George's Fina, turn right (east) on Woodrow Road and continue past the stop signs at 20th Street and Industrial Drive. Cross Industrial Drive and the railroad tracks. After crossing the tracks, stay to the left at the Y intersection, then take the next right. This road, which may not be posted but is known as Golf Course Road, winds beside the **Slaton Municipal Golf Course.** You will be traveling north and will soon drop into **Horseshoe Bend Canyon.** This can be a dazzling descent, but be especially careful in damp weather. There is a sharp curve in this steep downhill which is blind to oncoming traffic.

Continue north through the only tree tunnel in the county and up the other side of the canyon. This is a long climb, but not too steep. After you come out of the canyon, the road turns to the west. Look for the oil pump jacks along the road. The oil industry is a mainstay of the area's economy and more stable (even though depressed) now than it was in the boom and bust days of the 1920s and 1930s. Stay to the left at the Y intersection and continue until you reach the stop sign at FM 400. Turn left and you will begin to enjoy the rugged beauty of the canyons.

These canyons have been used for hundreds of centuries by the Indians who hunted here. Before the European horse was introduced in the late sixteenth century, the abundant buffalo and antelope could be trapped in the upper reaches of the canyons and speared to death. After the Plains tribes acquired the horse, buffalo were often stampeded over the cliffs of the canyons and butchered near the springs. The 200-acre lake known as Buffalo Springs is named for this practice. Today, the lake is a popular place for fishing, boating, hiking, and camping. Showers, full hookups, paddle boats, a convenience store and cafe, water slide, and crappie house add to the enjoyment of the lake.

The upcoming canyon is a long, relatively easy descent and climb with enchanting views on both sides of the road. Continue on FM 400 for 4.5 miles and turn right (west) just before you reach the **Slaton Airport.** Ride for 3.7 miles, cross the railroad tracks, and turn right (west) on U.S. 84. After 1.3 miles, turn right onto FM 835 and head north for 2 miles. If you began your ride at Buffalo Springs Lake, continue north to the park entrance. If you started in Slaton, turn left on FM 3020 to proceed with the ride by the feedyards.

During your visit to the Lubbock area you will also want to see the **Science Spectrum,** a museum featuring over 100 hands-on, up-to-the-minute scientific exhibits, the **Texas Tech University Museum** and **Moody Planetarium,** and **Reese Air Force Base jet pilot training center.**

ACCOMMODATIONS: Lubbock Plaza Motel, 3201 South Loop 289, Lubbock, (806) 797-3241. **Slaton Motor Inn,** Highway 84 Bypass, P.O. Box 355, Slaton, (806) 828-5831.

CAMPING: Buffalo Springs Lake, Lake Ranger's office, Lubbock, (806) 747-0496. **KOA Campground,** Clovis Highway, Lubbock, (806) 762-8653.

FOR MORE INFORMATION: Lubbock Chamber of Commerce, P.O. Box 561, Lubbock, Texas, 79408, (806) 763-4666.

LOCAL BIKE SHOPS: Bike Korner, Too, 2002 34th Street, Lubbock, (806) 763-2515. **Hutchinson's Cycles and Fitness,** 4210 82nd Street, Lubbock, (806) 792-7131. **South Plains Schwinn,** 4602 34th Street, Lubbock, (806) 792-9105.

The Quitaque
Canyon Loop

The beauty and immensity of the escarpment area assault all the senses and leave you entranced. Can you imagine looking at millions of years in one glance? Surely, you think, this dramatic exposure resulted from some cataclysm, an earthquake, maybe. No, a few tiny creeks and eons of time created this landscape. The sunrise brings the cliffs and canyons to life, breathing with the breeze, in colors you can hardly imagine and will want to try to remember. With each minute the shadows change and the scene shimmers with new hues. The Caprock marks the division of the Llano Estacado to the west and the rolling central plains to the east, with a change in elevation of 1,100 feet.

While not a journey to the center of the earth, this is surely a journey to the beginning of time on earth. The deep red to red-brown and red to green beds are from the Permian layer, dating back to 250 million years ago. There are white, usually horizontal veins of gypsum interlaced in these rocks. (Any water that has filtered through this salty stuff is unfit to drink, so be sure to bring water with you.) This Paleozoic era was rich in plant life, with fish and amphibians as the dominant fauna. But the stage was set for the most dramatic scene in the evolutionary play, the Mesozoic era: The age of dinosaurs. The Triassic period rocks make up the characteristic canyon landscape. These are the blocky sandstones that sheer off in vertical sheets under erosion. The vividly colorful stripes of grayish green to lavender-yellow shales are also Triassic. As a point of reference, the first dinosaurs developed during this time.

- **Starting point:** Caprock Canyons State Park (loop)
- **Mileage:** 58.5 miles
- **Terrain:** Gently rolling to rolling climbs
- **Best time to ride:** April through early November
- **Traffic conditions:** light
- **Road conditions:** good with wide shoulder on Highway 86

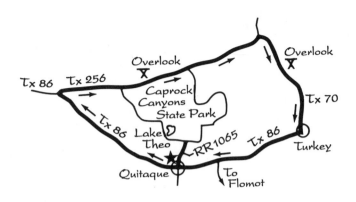

Another feature of the Triassic formations are the abundant inlays of chert, jasper that the early native hunters used to craft their spear points and arrowheads. Native Americans have used the canyon areas for 12,000 years, beginning with their migration from Siberia after the retreat of glaciers from the last Ice Age. These first people hunted the giant horned bison, mastodon, giant ground sloth, camel, and native horse to extinction. Later, the smaller buffalo became the mainstay of these Plains tribes.

Over the next several thousand years, successively more developed cultures used the area. Recorded history began when Coronado encountered nomadic tribes of Teya and Querecho. After the Apache bands acquired the European horse, they became preeminent hunters, following the bison herds across millions of square miles of plains. The most fierce of the Plains tribes became the Comanche. They were peaceful Shoshone farmers until they acquired the horse, and they very nearly kept this domain for their own. Many artifacts, spear points, tools, and utensils of these native cultures have been recovered from this area.

The Quitaque (pronounced kit'-a-kway) Canyon Loop ride is approximately 58.5 miles through moderately rugged terrain on good roads. Allow half a day for the ride so you'll have plenty of time to stop and take photographs of the area. Although April through early November are the best times to do the ride, especially if you plan to camp, many winter days will be just warm enough for an enjoyable trip. This loop can begin from the **Caprock Canyons State Park,** three miles north of **Quitaque,** or from the **Hotel Turkey** (in **Turkey**). Begin by heading west on State Highway 86 toward **Silverton.**

This is an excellent road for cycling with a 12-foot shoulder and very little truck traffic. From Turkey, the first leg of the loop begins with 10 miles of gently rolling swells between stretches of smooth, flat road. The next 14 miles from Quitaque includes a rolling climb of about 970 feet.

In the years following the first Spanish explorations of the escarpment area, the *comancheros* (traders) met with the Plains Indians along a trade route through here, and eventually a trading post was established at the present site of Quitaque. During the years just following the Civil War, *cibolleros* (buffalo hunters) brought in mountains of hides which were shipped to Santa Fe and St. Louis. In 1890, the town became a stagecoach stop.

Look for redwing blackbirds, scissortail flycatchers, and meadowlarks along with the ever-present mourning doves and mockingbirds. You might also spot a golden eagle or ring neck pheasant, or one of the other 175 species often sighted here. Spring and early summer are the best times to view the plentiful wildflowers and butterflies.

Just before you get to Silverton, the route turns to the right and you'll ride for 19.2 miles on State Highway 256. You'll be traveling through rich farmland: cotton, grain crops, and winter wheat stretch to the horizon in all directions.

Shortly, you'll descend the Caprock and the flat farmland of the Llano Estacado turns into the canyons and arroyos of the escarpment. There are two picnic spots along this stretch of road, both of which offer great photo opportunities.

Red ear sliders, snapping turtles, and box turtles with their brown and yellow swirled shells are abundant, especially near the creek beds. The iridescent blue-green flashes you will see are prairie lined racerunners, active daytime lizards. Other lizards inhabit the area, including the Great Plains skink and the spotted whiptail, but you're not likely to see these from your bicycle. Horned toads are evident in warm weather. They are harmless, but don't pick them up because they have a nasty habit of squirting blood out of their eyes when stressed! You may see a variety of snakes (most are harmless but watch for rattlesnakes) along the road, especially from May through October.

Turn right on State Highway 70 and head south for 13.1 miles back into Turkey. You'll be traveling down the arroyo of the **Little Red River.** The successive layers of exposed rock are magnificent. Near the tops of the canyon walls are sedimentary rocks over a thick layer of caliche. Triassic period rocks (with inlays of chert so prized by early Native cultures) lay just over the red Permian layer.

One hundred years ago, you would have seen hundreds of wild turkeys along the creeks. Early white settlers eradicated the flocks by 1905, but they have been reintroduced and are gaining a foothold. The town of Turkey was originally known as Turkey Roost, before the postal service shortened its name.

Small mammals seen frequently include ground squirrels, cottontail rabbits, coyotes, and skunks. Also inhabiting the area are porcupine, raccoon, bobcat, mule deer, and Aoudad "sheep" (actually African sand goats, introduced to promote commercial hunting).

If your ride began from Caprock Canyons State Park, you will turn right at the **Allsup's** convenience store in Turkey to take State Highway 86 back to the park.

Turkey is now a sleepy hamlet serving the needs of the surrounding farming area. But when the Santa Fe railroad came through in 1927, this was a bustling commercial center. A $50,000 two-story brick hotel was built to serve the farmers and cattlemen who came to ship their crops and cows. Drummers used the rooms to sell their wares from trunks before traveling on to the next stop.

During the 1930s, the hotel dining room became the springboard for Bob Wills' leap into musical history with his famous Western-swing sound. Fans and music lovers flock to Turkey the last weekend in April each year to celebrate **Bob Wills' Day.**

The railroad is gone now but the historic Hotel Turkey is still going strong. Jane and Scott Johnson bought the hotel in 1988, and have redecorated the rooms using pieces of the original furniture and evocative chintz and lace to recreate the nostalgic flavor of the place. Speaking of flavor, homecooked meals are a special treat in the 40-seat dining room. Jane often has a story to tell, or a local fiddler or banjo picker is likely to stop by.

The Hotel Turkey is included on the National Register of Historic Places, and is a Texas Historical Property. Stop for an hour to learn more about this Western heritage.

Caprock Canyons State Park is located 3 miles north of Quitaque on Ranch Road 1065 and covers almost 14,000 acres of some of the most picturesque bluffs and badlands anywhere. **Lake Theo** provides swimming and fishing fun. There are extensive hiking trails (worth the effort), camping, day-use areas and picnic areas, and an amphitheater for educational programs and slide shows. For off-road enthusiasts, there are now several miles of single-track trails open and more are planned for the near future. For more information write to the Park Superintendent at Caprock Canyons State Park.

ACCOMMODATIONS: Hotel Turkey, P.O. Box 37, Turkey, 1-800-657-7110.

CAMPING: Caprock Canyons State Park, P.O. Box 204, Quitaque, (806) 455-1492.

FOR MORE INFORMATION: Quitaque Chamber of Commerce, P.O. Box 427, Quitaque, Texas, 79255, (806) 455-1456.

The Canyon Loop

Canyon (named for the magnificent **Palo Duro Canyon** just to the east of town) was originally the headquarters for the gigantic **T-Anchor ranch.** In 1877, Leigh Dyer, whose brother-in-law was the famous traildriver and pioneer rancher Charles Goodnight, drove 400 head of cattle to this claim. The log cabin he built of juniper from the Palo Duro Canyon is still sound and is a part of the **Panhandle Plains Historical Museum** at **West Texas State University.**

Dyer started his ranch only three years after the last major Indian battle in Texas. Feeling their treaties had been dismissed, marauding Comanches had left their reservations in Oklahoma and threatened a wide territory. Colonel Ranald S. Mackenzie led the 4th Calvary on a surprise raid, in which they captured and slaughtered 1,400 horses and burned the Indian village. With no shelter, provisions, or transportation, the feared and respected Comanches resigned themselves to reservation life and walked back to Oklahoma.

Cattle ranching is still a dominant industry here. The area feeds and ships over 4 million head yearly, many from the feedyards dotting the region. Gently rolling pastures are interspersed with cultivated fields of small grains and sugar beets irrigated with abundant underground water. Modern travelers succumb to the seduction of the vast landscapes and colorful sunsets that first drew the young Georgia O'Keefe to the West. In 1916 she wrote, "It is absurd how much I love this country."

One attraction you can't miss on your trip to Canyon is an excursion to Palo Duro Canyon. With over 15,000 acres of dramatic

- **Starting point:** Canyon
- **Mileage:** 57 miles
- **Terrain:** flat
- **Best time to ride:** late September through mid-April
- **Traffic conditions:** very light, except on U.S. 60
- **Road conditions:** fair

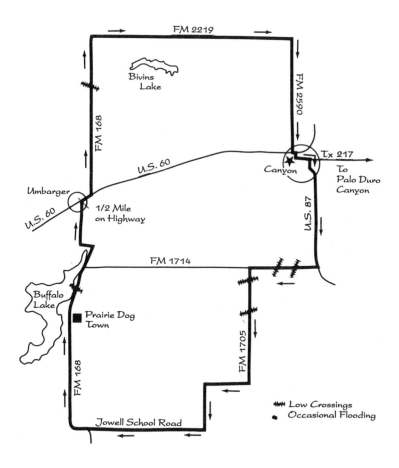

scenery, the Grand Canyon of Texas, as it is often called, is breathtaking. Early morning and late afternoon provide some spectacular photography opportunities as the strata of the canyon walls mingle, producing a rhapsody of color.

Pulitzer Prize winner Paul Green's fascinating outdoor musical drama, *Texas,* performed from late June through late August every day except Sundays, is worth a special trip. Other attractions in the canyon are the **Sad Monkey Railroad** and the **Goodnight Trading Post** as well as camping, hiking, and horseback riding.

This 57-mile loop will be enjoyable for any rider, but for naturalists and birders, it is a "must do." Most of the route is on well-maintained but narrow farm roads, with very little traffic. Late September through mid-April are the best months to see the millions of migrating waterfowl, but there are many other birds and wildlife visible year-round. If you have younger riders in your party, they are sure to be delighted by the bird watching.

The ride begins on the south side of Canyon, from the Dairy Queen at 13th Avenue and Highway 87 (23rd Street). Head south on Highway 87 for 4 miles. Turn right (west) on FM 1714 for 3 miles. Infrequent but heavy rainfall may cause creeks that are normally dry to run over the road. You may want to portage your bike across these places because you are unable to see any debris in the muddy water.

Turn left (south) on FM 1705. These farm roads are very well maintained, but they are narrow and you may need to keep to the extreme right side of the road to accommodate large machinery. You will probably see some small mammals: skunks, prairie dogs, ground squirrels, and rabbits. The two kinds of rabbits you're most likely to see are the jackrabbit (actually a hare), with very large squared-off ears, and the much smaller cottontail (a true rabbit) with short legs. When frightened, a jackrabbit may leap two car lengths at a time to escape; a cottontail will scamper away in a zig-zag pattern using any bushes or rocks for cover.

After 5 miles, the main road turns sharply to the right and a secondary road goes straight; stay on the main road. About 2 miles later, turn left and ride south for 2 more miles. There is a solitary square brick building on the left and you will turn right at the Jowell School Road (you should be at about 16 miles into the ride). This road is marked, but not numbered.

You will be riding west, mostly through pastureland. Herds of cattle, moved from pasture to pasture throughout the year, will be all around. You may be surprised to see buffalo (actually bison) in the pastures. They are no longer wild, but are raised as part of a conservation plan to reestablish this nearly extinct giant.

After 5.5 miles, this road will merge with FM 168. Be sure to merge carefully because 168 curves at this juncture and motorists may not see you. For the next 10 miles you will be skirting the eastern edge of **Buffalo Lake National Wildlife Refuge.** Expect to see an astonishing variety and number of birds. If you would like a leaflet listing the birds of the area, write to the refuge manager at P.O. Box 179, Umbarger, Texas, 79091.

Native year-round birds you're almost certain to see are the redwinged blackbird, one of the easiest birds to recognize because of its bright red shoulder patches; mourning dove; mockingbird; ring-necked pheasant; bobwhite quail; chaparral (roadrunners); Swainson's and red-tailed hawks. The big birds sitting humped on telephone poles or sailing in grand circles overhead are not properly the "buzzards" of wagon train fame, but turkey vultures. Similar in flight and size are the great golden eagles, which are even larger. Turkey vultures soar with wings in a slight V while golden eagles hold their wings horizontally. At rest, you can identify a turkey vulture because it has a red head; the golden eagle is more tan to yellow colored.

This area is the southern part of the central flyway where millions of waterfowl migrate each spring and fall—eighty thousand Canadian geese and snow geese winter here. Easily identifiable ducks are the colorful teals, green- and blue-winged as well as the cinnamon, mallard, and redhead. You'll probably have to drive into the refuge itself to see buffleheads or mergansers, but with over 30 duck and geese species present during different times of the year, it's worth the drive.

As you look to the west, you may see deer grazing. Most are the smaller white-tail, but there are heavier mule deer in the area also. You may also see pronghorn "antelope" (actually closer relatives to sheep than antelope) running gracefully through the arroyos.

About 7.5 miles from the merge onto FM 168, there is an educational walking trail at the prairie dog town. This is about the halfway point of the ride, and you will enjoy the zany antics of these small brown clowns. Continue on FM 168 into **Umbarger** and turn right onto U.S. 60. This is an extremely busy highway with much truck traffic, so be exceptionally careful. This is the only half mile that you won't be able to gawk!

Turn left—proceed north across U.S. 60, being very careful—onto Highway 168 and continue. You can relax now, and enjoy the windmill turning lazily in the distance. After 5 miles, turn to the right with the main road. Just ahead on the right, but not quite visible from this road is **Bivins Lake.** Here you may see sandhill cranes, white-faced ibis, American avocets, ring-billed seagulls, and several species of sandpipers. But unless you have your field guide, it may not be easy to distinguish between them.

For the next 5 miles you'll see more houses and trees along the road. Look for crow and grackle, both black birds. Providing more colorful sightings are blue jays, robins, cardinals, meadowlarks, and blue grosbeaks (only the males are blue).

Turn right at the golf course on FM 2590 and you're on the final 5-mile stretch. There is a bit more traffic on this road, but you'll still be able to enjoy the scenery. When you intersect with Highway 60, (again, be careful) cross all the way over to the access road and turn left. About one-quarter mile ahead is a stop sign, where you will turn right.

These next directions may seem bewildering because both the streets and the avenues are numbered, but there aren't any quirky turns. If you get confused, or think you're lost, just ask someone how to get to the Dairy Queen. Canyon is a small town and the people are friendly. The right turn at the stop sign puts you on 11th Street. Go to 4th Avenue and turn left. Go to 19th Street and turn right (at the Methodist church), riding to 12th Avenue. If you started from the park, you've reached your destination. If you started from the Dairy Queen, continue around the park. Turn left on 12th Avenue, go one block, turn right on 20th Street, continue one more block and turn left. Dairy Queen will be just ahead.

ACCOMMODATIONS: Hudspeth House (bed and breakfast), 1905 4th Avenue, Canyon, (806) 655-9800. **Goodnight Inn,** Route 2 Box 142, Canyon, 1-800-654-7350. **Hampton Inn,** 1700 I-40 East, Amarillo, 1-800-416-7866. **Best Western,** 830 West First Street, Hereford, (806) 364-0540.

CAMPING: Buffalo Lake National Wildlife Refuge, P.O. Box 228, Umbarger, (806) 499-3382 or (806) 499-3254. **Palo Duro Canyon State Park,** Route 2 Box 285, Canyon, (806) 488-2227.

FOR MORE INFORMATION: Amarillo Chamber of Commerce, P.O. Box 9480, Amarillo, Texas, 79106, (806) 373-7800.

LOCAL BIKE SHOPS: Bike Korner, 1739 Avendale Shopping Center, Amarillo, (806) 355-9408. **Hills Sports Shop,** 4021 Mockingbird, Amarillo, (806) 355-7224. **Mason's Pro Frame Shop,** 3333 South Coulter, Amarillo, (806) 359-3826.

SOUTH TEXAS PLAINS AND SEASHORE

• • •

Ann K. Baird

I won't kid you—South Texas is an acquired taste. It takes time and a passion for open spaces to understand a land that is at once inviting and unforgiving, graced with opulence and nagged by poverty. At times, the land is lush with vegetation and wildflowers; at others it is parched, with its trees, plants, and animals struggling to survive. Those who love South Texas pride themselves on the mettle it takes to appreciate landscapes that aren't classical, towns that are functional rather than quaint.

Of course, many love it for the richness of its natural resources: oil and gas, vast grazing lands, river valleys, and wildlife. The wildlife is what draws hunters from all over the country to chase native Texas white-tail deer, quail, dove, wild turkeys, ducks, and geese. Fishermen seek bass, striper, and catfish in the rivers and reservoirs, and speckled trout, red-fish, and flounder in the coastal bays.

South Texas could be defined as the horn-shaped part of the state lying south of old Highway 90. Ecologically, though, the region defies one characterization. Within those boundaries, you'll find coastline and barrier islands, deserts, farms and ranch land, and fertile river valleys, the most notable of which is the Rio Grande Valley, known everywhere in Texas simply as The Valley. The following tours will take you through each of these distinct South Texas regions.

Texas Freedom Trail Tour

Six countries fought three wars and many more skirmishes in this area, over its abundance of agricultural and grazing lands and its network of navigable waterways that leads to the Gulf. This geographic juxtaposition led to the establishment of several Spanish missions between here and San Antonio, and the area is still referred to as Mission Valley. The landscapes blend South Texas ruggedness and East Texas greenery; moss-draped oaks coexist with cacti and century plants.

Although the climate here is temperate enough to allow year-round cycling, you're better off avoiding July and August when the heat and humidity make it a challenge just to take your bike off the car-top rack. The terrain is kinder—mostly flat, with a few rolls here and there.

The city of **Victoria,** the beginning and ending point of this loop tour, rivals some of the more well-known port cities of the South with its charming historic district and beautifully maintained old homes. Although you won't see a sign of salt water, Victoria is actually a port with access to the Gulf and the Intercoastal Waterway via the 35-mile long Victoria Canal. This, plus its proximity to vast ranch lands—Victoria is only a 100 miles or so from the famed King Ranch—accounted for its prosperity in the years after the Texas Revolution. Later, oil and gas exploration and the growth of the chemical industry boosted Victoria's economy.

Unfortunately, growth has brought inevitable suburban sprawl, so I recommend donning blinders for the hellish stretch of malls and franchise fooderies you'll pass as you enter the city. Head straight for the **Historic District,** which is neatly designated by special street signs

- **Starting point:** Victoria (loop)
- **Mileage:** 62 miles (with options)
- **Terrain:** flat to rolling
- **Best time to ride:** September through June
- **Traffic conditions:** moderate
- **Road conditions:** good

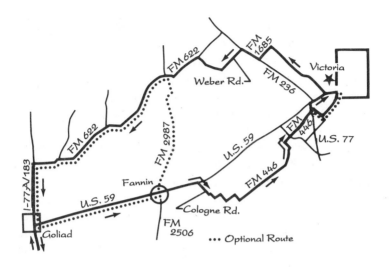

marking the original townsite laid out in 1824 by Martin DeLeon, the first to colonize the area. The difference between this section and the rest of the city is as palpable as if you tripped a laser beam. The streets get quieter, shadier; the architecture grows more intriguing. Nearly 100 buildings and homes in this area are listed in the National Register of Historic Places, so the best way to appreciate this architectural treasure chest is to obtain a free copy of the convention bureau's pamphlet, *Walking and Driving Tour of Old Victoria.* Because the bureau is closed on weekends, you might want to write or call for a copy in advance. The entire tour is longer than you might want to walk, but not as enjoyable by auto, so it makes a delightful bike ramble.

If you don't have time to take the entire tour, at least reserve some time to visit **DeLeon Plaza,** where a grove of trees shade a gazebo and some benches—a lovely place to stretch out after your ride—and the adjacent **Victoria County Courthouse,** which was built in 1892, is the finest example of Richardson Romanesque style in Texas. The old clock still chimes reliably on the hour, and the upstairs courtroom has been restored to its original decor. Next, ride through the neighborhoods bordering downtown. Here are blocks and blocks of what I call Gulf Coast Victorians, two-storied white clapboards with side cupolas and pillared verandas designed originally to soothe their occupants through an unairconditioned August.

Victoria matches its historic grandeur with an impish sense of humor. The last weekend in October, Victoria holds its **International Armadillo Confab and Exposition,** which has been going on since the value of armadillos was just beginning to be appreciated. The admission to the exposition makes a droll statement on the times: 25 cents or a barrel of crude oil. The rest of the events spoof small town festivals everywhere: a Miss Vacant Lot beauty contest, King Bubba contest, Jalapeño Gobble, Whimmy Diddle-Off (it's worth going just to find out what that is!) and, of course, the armadillo races. Slightly more conventional offerings include a chili cook-off, arts and crafts booths, and entertainment.

When you are ready to begin your ride, proceed to **Riverside Park,** a 562-acre city park on the banks of the Guadalupe River, just off Highway 59/77 South near the historic district (watch for the signs). Although this park doesn't allow overnight camping, it's the best place to park your car. You can also stop at the **Texas Zoo,** which features native Texas wildlife exclusively and is involved in the preservation of endangered Texas' species. The zoo is open seven days a week; call (512) 573-7681 for more information. From near the zoo, follow Memorial Drive out of the park. It will become Stayton Drive. Continue on Stayton Drive to Vine Street, which is the last street before you hit Highway 59/77 and turn right. Follow Vine Street, which parallels the highway, to Water Street and turn left. You must then turn right on Highway 59/77 to cross the bridge over the Guadalupe River. Use extreme caution here! The bridge, although two lanes wide, is narrow and the traffic will be heavy.

Once you're across, the road widens, and there's a good shoulder. Follow Highway 59/77 1.2 miles to the first stoplight. This is FM 1685; turn right. Follow this through a sea of cotton, corn, and grain fields to FM 236 and turn right. Go 1.6 miles until you come to a gas station/store. Turn left just before the store on Weber Road. This winds through a ranch, and thus has cattle guards and a few other rough patches, but is otherwise lovely and traffic-free. After 4.4 miles, Weber Road will make a T intersection with FM 622. Turn left and follow it to **Schroeder** (pronounced "Schrader," like the valve). There probably won't be any stores open here.

Follow FM 622 for 12 more miles until it hits Highway 77/183. Turn left toward **Goliad,** 4.5 miles away. This is a busy, major north-south thoroughfare, but it has a good shoulder. When you pull into Goliad, you'll cross Highway 59. There's the usual small town smattering of stores and cafes here, but don't stop yet. Continue on through this intersection until you see the sign to **Historic Downtown,** just a couple of blocks down on the right.

If you're ready for lunch, you might try the **Empresario Restaurant,** which is open for lunch seven days a week and features sandwiches and Mexican food specials. Stroll around the square, admire the old stone courthouse and check out the **Hanging Tree** on the north side. After trial and conviction in the courthouse, the culprits were led out and summarily hung from the branches of the large live oak out front, inevitably decreasing the repeat-offender problem.

Then, continue back to Highway 77 and turn right (south) toward the **Presidio La Bahia, Zaragoza birthplace,** and the **Mission Espiritu Santo de Zuniga,** on the grounds of **Goliad State Park.** You'll come to Goliad State Historic Park headquarters first, on the right, about 1 mile outside Goliad. The entire park is located in four parcels spread out around the area. At this location, you can swim (there's a pool on park premises), hike, or picnic and explore the old Mission Espiritu Santo building. The mission was originally founded in 1722 on the banks of Matagorda Bay but finally relocated to this site on the **San Antonio River** in 1749 to educate, civilize, and proselytize the Native Americans in the area. After falling into disrepair around the turn of the century, it was renovated in 1936 by the Civilian Conservation Corps.

Across the San Antonio River, about a mile further down Highway 77 from the park headquarters, is the fully restored Presidio La Bahia and museum. This was the mission's companion military fort, and served as military headquarters for all the changing governments that occupied the area. Its most tragic hour came during the Texas Revolution in 1836, when it was the site of the Goliad massacre. Following Colonel James Fannin's surrender at the Battle of Coleto Creek (about 8 miles east of here), his men were imprisoned at the Presidio. Under the terms of the surrender, they were to be treated as prisoners of war according to standards generally accepted by the civilized nations of the world, and they were to be transferred to the United States border. Upon hearing this, the 400 Texans, most of whom were from elsewhere in the United States anyway, struck up a chorus of "Home Sweet Home." A week later, on Palm Sunday, they were marched out of the Presidio and shot. Interestingly, while the Alamo has captured the world's attention, and indeed has become an icon of Texas, it was this travesty that really inflamed the Texans and pressured Sam Houston to advance and confront Santa Ana.

The Presidio today includes a chapel and museum, and a completely reconstructed fortress complex. The chapel interior is simple, with arched masonry walls reminiscent of Spanish mission construction of that era, and a mural, painted much later, that portrays Jesus walking among the local cactus and rattlesnakes. Behind the Presidio is the **Fannin Monument and Grave,** where the remains of the massacred men are buried.

Adjacent to the Presidio is the birthplace of Ignacio Zaragoza, the Mexican general who was born and reared here. During the Battle of Puebla, during Mexico's war to overthrow the French, Zaragoza's badly outnumbered forces defeated an army of veteran French Zoaves. The victory occurred on May 5, 1862, giving rise to the Mexican national holiday Cinco de Mayo.

To continue your ride, retrace the short distance on Highway 77/183 to Goliad and to the intersection of Highway 77/183 and Highway 59. Turn right on Highway 59 toward **Fannin** and Victoria. This is a major highway, but has an excellent shoulder and the traffic is surprisingly manageable, although you're sure to encounter your share of 18-wheelers. If you don't find riding here unpleasant, you can continue the entire way to Victoria, 24 miles away, shortening your ride by about 4 miles.

I recommend, however, that you turn right on Cologne Road, 3.2 miles on Highway 59 past the little community of Fannin. You'll have to watch carefully for this turn, which is only marked by a street sign. Cologne Road winds around for 2.8 miles and Ts into an unmarked road. Turn left here. Follow this for 1.4 miles and watch carefully for FM 446, which cuts to the left. There's no warning junction sign for this road, which is surprising, because it turns out to be a good backroad.

FM 446 slices through typically flat coastal prairie land toward Victoria. You'll continue on it for 13 miles, crossing a major intersection with Loop 175 at 12.5 miles, until it dead-ends into Timber Drive. Turn left here to hit Highway 59 immediately and then turn right on Highway 59 to retrace your route across the Guadalupe bridge back into Riverside Park. If you're not tired yet and prefer a more rural ride back into town, you can turn right on Timber, which will dead-end into a road that runs through a city park. Turn left, and follow this road around through an unexpected forest until it hits River Road. Turn left and then veer immediately right (you'll see Highway 59 from here) and turn right on Highway 59 just south of the bridge.

Route Options: If you want to shorten this route, but still hit all the points of interest, begin and end the ride in Schroeder (park near the Dance Hall). Take the same route to Goliad as the one described above. From Goliad, proceed to Fannin on Highway 59. Turn left on FM 2987 and follow it for 8 miles back to Schroeder. This makes the ride 41 miles.

ACCOMMODATIONS: Best Western Inn, 2605 Houston Highway (U.S. 59), Victoria, (512) 578-9911. **Chaparral Motel,** 3401 East Loop 175, Victoria, (512) 576-9222. **Holiday Inn,** 2705 Houston Highway (U.S. 59), Victoria, (512) 575-0251. **Ramada Inn,** 3901 Houston Highway (U.S. 59), Victoria, (512) 578-2723. **Motel 6,** 3716 Houston Highway (U.S. 59), (512) 573-1273. **The Dial House** (bed and breakfast), 306 West Oak Street, Goliad, (512) 645-3366. **The Madison** (bed and breakfast), P.O. Box 963, on Highway 183 (Cuero Highway), Goliad, (512) 645-8693.

CAMPING: Victoria RV Park (run by Victoria Parks and Recreation Department), on Vine Street near Red River Street, Victoria, (512) 572-2763. **Spring Creek RV Park,** at Highway 87 and Raab Road, Victoria, (512) 575-3651. **Coleto Creek Reservoir and Park,** P.O. Drawer 68 (on Highway 59 between Goliad and Victoria) Fannin, (512) 575-6366.

FOR MORE INFORMATION: Victoria Chamber of Commerce, 700 Main Center, Suite 101, Victoria, Texas, 77901, (512) 573-5277.

LOCAL BIKE SHOPS: Bill's Bikes, 505 East North Street, Victoria, (512) 575-6036.

Texas' Playground Day Ride

For cyclists there's good news and bad news about **Corpus Christi,** the delightful city at the northern end of Texas' great barrier landmark, **Padre Island.** The good news is that the city has made some wonderful additions and renovations to its downtown and bayfront area; the bad news is that many of them are inaccessible to bicycles. If you're into solitary beachcombing, **Padre Island National Park and Seashore** beckons with miles of uncrowded, undeveloped beach. But to get to it you have to cross JFK Causeway, and crossing it on a bicycle would be sporting at best.

What makes bicycle touring around Corpus Christi, and indeed much of the Texas coast, so difficult is the necklace of causeways (overpasses over bays and estuaries) that connect the barrier islands just off the Texas mainland. These causeways were designed and built solely for the automobile (the only way too many Texans seem to enjoy going anywhere). Many of them appear unnavigable even by pedestrians—heaven help you if your car breaks down—and because bridges of any kind are so expensive to build, there are no alternative, less trafficked bypasses.

Nonetheless, Corpus Christi has so much to offer—in my opinion it's one of the loveliest cities on the Texas Coast—that I still believe it warrants inclusion in an overview of South Texas. There are tricks to getting around, but Corpus Christi sports a young athletic population, so bicycles are becoming more common sights. A ride along the bay on Ocean Drive on a quiet, sunny Sunday morning will more than reward you for your efforts.

- **Starting point:** Corpus Christi (loop)
- **Mileage:** 22 miles
- **Terrain:** rolling
- **Best time to ride:** good year-round (in winter, check weather conditions)
- **Traffic conditions:** heavy at times (lightest on weekend mornings)
- **Road conditions:** fair

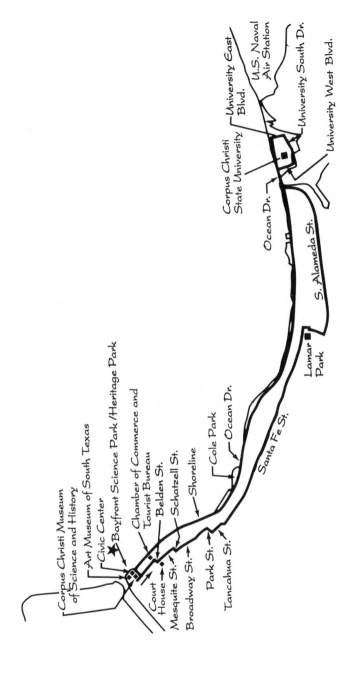

Corpus Christi forms a crescent around the bay of the same name which was discovered by Spanish explorer Alonso Alvarez de Pineda in 1519. Because he made landfall on the religious holiday of Corpus Christi (the Body of Christ), he named the bay after it. Corpus Christi didn't take hold as a community until 300 years later when a trading post was set up near the mouth of the bay.

Begin your ride at **Bayfront Science Park,** at the northwest end of Shoreline Boulevard. You can park your car at the parking lot for the Civic Center and auditorium, and spend a little time exploring the park complex. Also located here is the **Corpus Christi Museum of Science and History,** where you can climb aboard the wreck of a Spanish ship or learn about the training of U.S. Navy pilots (a naval air station is located in Corpus Christi). In addition to the exhibits, the museum is a good place to stock up on brochures and information if the convention and visitor's bureau is closed.

Next door is the **Art Museum of South Texas,** a stark, contemporary building with a glass side for a full view of the bay. The glass is all tinted, however, so as to protect and not to distort the colors of the artwork on display. There are a small eclectic permanent collection and traveling exhibits. Both this and the Science and History Museum are open every day except Monday and holidays. Call (512) 883-2862 for more information.

Across a narrow channel of the bay is the **Texas State Aquarium,** which focuses on aquatic ecosystems of the Gulf of Mexico and the Caribbean Sea. It's well worth a visit but, unfortunately, to get to it you must cross the **Harbor Bridge,** the impressive iron span structure that curves directly over Bayfront Science Park. Crossing the Harbor Bridge by bicycle would be risky. You'll want to lock your bike at the Bayfront park complex and take one of the fish-painted city buses that runs along the bayfront to the aquarium.

From Bayfront Park, go left on Chaparral to **Heritage Park,** a collection of renovated homes adjacent to Bayfront Park. The homes were purchased and moved to this site by various organizations in the city. The homes range from the functional to the extravagant. Notable is the **Sidbury House,** painstakingly restored by the Corpus Christi Junior League with wallpaper hand printed in Europe in accordance with the original Victorian design. All the homes on display are within a three-block area. The visiting hours of the homes vary, so you might want to get a copy of the walking tour of Heritage Park brochure available at the **Galvan House.**

One-half mile after Heritage Park, turn right on Belden Street and left on Mesquite Street past the **Old Nueces County Courthouse,** which is in disrepair. Built in 1914, this neoclassical structure once served as a shelter during "Carla," the worst of the hurricanes to hit Corpus Christi. Continue on Belden Street through the downtown business district to Schatzell Street (or Schatzel, depending on which street sign you see) and turn right. This curves to the left and climbs the only significant hill on the tour to Upper Broadway Street. Before you climb all the way, check out the restored sculpture in front of the little fountain near this curve. This is Pompeo Coppini's 1914 sculpture *Queen of the Sea*.

You will be climbing up **The Bluff,** once a distinctive landmark between the downtown business district and the uptown residential area. In the early 1900s, a beautification project added the curved masonry staircases, the white railing, and a number of memorials along the route. The upper street is Upper Broadway, the lower portion, Lower Broadway.

As you curve up the hill, you'll be on Upper Broadway; turn left. This street is narrow and tends to have lots of parked cars along the side, so use caution. You'll pass **St. Patrick's Cathedral,** which began with a congregation that formed in 1853, and the **Centennial House,** the oldest surviving house in the city that also served as a hospital during the Civil War. The house is open for tours only on Wednesday afternoons, or by appointment. Call (512) 992-6003 for more information.

Follow North Upper Broadway until it appears to dead-end at a confusing intersection. Actually, there are three streets emanating from this point. Veer right to continue on what becomes South Upper Broadway. You'll pass the **Episcopal Church of the Good Shepherd.** Turn right on Park, just past the church, and turn left on Tancahua Street.

Follow Tancahua Street until it veers to the right and becomes Santa Fe Street. Santa Fe Street becomes more residential as you leave downtown Corpus Christi and enter one of its older neighborhoods, developed in the 1920s. On the left are some particularly pretty streets, bisected by wide, boulevard-type islands, common to several of the neighborhoods in Corpus Christi.

Approximately 3.5 miles after Tancahua Street becomes Santa Fe Street, turn right on Circle Street, which jogs around **Lamar Park** and hits Alameda Street. Alameda Street is a slightly busier thoroughfare than Santa Fe Street, but it is four lanes wide. Follow Alameda Street past **Oso Beach Golf Course** until it hits into Ennis Joslin Road and splits. Turn, or veer, left. Very shortly thereafter, Ennis Joslin hits Ocean Drive. Turn right toward **Corpus Christi State University.**

Barely one-half mile after you turn onto Ocean Drive, you'll pass through the entrance of the university, located on a 250-acre island named, not surprisingly, University Island. Corpus Christi State, which offers a two-year upper-level program and graduate school with an enrollment of nearly 4,000, is now part of the Texas A&M System. It is the home of the Center for Coastal Studies and the National Spill Control School, where students learn the latest techniques for handling all types of hazardous-material spills.

Turn right into the campus on University West Boulevard and follow it to University South Drive and turn left. Turn left again onto University East Boulevard and follow it back to Ocean Drive. Turn left. If you want to get a glimpse of the **Corpus Christi Naval Air Station,** you may turn right here, but you'll be turned back at the gate, 1.75 miles down.

At any rate, you'll have to turn around eventually and begin riding west/northwest on Ocean Drive. You'll have the bay on your right, grand ocean front estates on your left, and if all is perfect, the wind at your back. There's even a bike lane of sorts on the far right, but watch for parked cars, inevitably belonging to those who thought it was a special beachfront parking space reserved just for them.

Watch for windsurfers along this stretch, but particularly at **Cole Park,** about 5 miles west of the university's entrance. With its consistent 15-to-25-mile-per-hour winds and warm bay waters, Corpus Christi is becoming a hotbed of windsurfing.

About 6 miles down, Ocean Front splits. You'll want to stay on the right fork, which becomes Shoreline Boulevard. To the right are marinas, floating restaurants, and a 20-foot wide seawall sidewalk that invites joggers, rollerbladers, and grandmas and kids in those funky pedal-powered surreys. From Shoreline, turn left on Hughes and right on Chaparral to return to Bayfront Park.

ACCOMMODATIONS: There are many hotels and condominiums in the area. To find accommodations best suited to your needs, contact the Corpus Christi Visitor's Bureau.

CAMPING: Padre Island National Seashore and Malaquite Beach, on Park Road 22 (25 miles south of the JFK Causeway), Corpus Christi, (512) 937-2621. **Mustang Island State Park,** on TX 361 (14 miles south of Port Aransas and 10 miles southeast of the JFK Causeway), Port Aransas, (512) 749-5246. **Padre Balli Park,** on Park Road 22 (7 miles southeast of the JFK Causeway), Corpus Christi, (512) 949-8121.

FOR MORE INFORMATION: Corpus Christi Convention and Visitor's Bureau, P.O. Box 2664, 1021 North Shoreline, Corpus Christi, Texas, 78403, (512) 882-5063 or 1-800-678-5232.

The Heart
of South Texas Ride

This ride, which begins and ends in the small community of **Three Rivers,** traverses quintessential Texas brush and ranch land. It will be an experience in the pure pleasure of being outside on your bicycle—there aren't many designated points of interest, except the big sky and the wildlife you'll encounter along the way. But the roads are all in fine condition, and the traffic should be very light.

Again the spring and fall are generally the best times to ride a bicycle anywhere in Texas, and this area is no exception to that rule. Spring takes a little precedence, because South Texas blossoms with a surprising variety of wildflowers and blooming cacti.

The time of day may make the most difference in this ride. If you want to see some wildlife, get out as soon after dawn as possible. If you have a keen eye, you will no doubt be rewarded with a glimpse of a fox, wild turkey, deer, armadillo, jackrabbit, cottontail, roadrunner, or rattlesnake. I was lucky enough once to roll up to a couple of gray foxes. One was in the middle of the road studying something (I never could quite figure out what) while his companion appeared to keep a lookout on the side. They were not the least bit skittish; indeed they eyed me with such cold confidence that I began to review my scant knowledge of how to behave in case of wildlife attack. Just then, I shifted my bicycle slightly and they darted off.

If you happen to be camped at Choke Canyon, you can begin this ride there, instead of at Three Rivers, because it is a loop tour that passes both those points. Three Rivers was founded by Charles Tips in the early 1900s on land he'd purchased from a Mrs. Hamilton. He con-

- **Starting point:** Three Rivers (loop)
- **Mileage:** 48 miles
- **Terrain:** gently rolling
- **Best time to ride:** March through June
- **Traffic conditions:** very light
- **Road conditions:** good

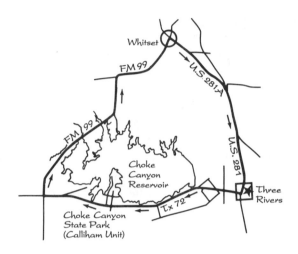

vinced her that he'd get the railroad to build a line here from San Antonio, and that if he succeeded, he'd name the town after her. He followed through on both counts, naming the town Hamiltonburg. But the post office complained that people frequently confused the name with the already established Hamilton, Texas, so Hamiltonburg became Three Rivers, named after the Atascosa, Frio, and Nueces rivers which merge here.

You can park your car in the square downtown and head out of town on Highway 72 west. (Highway 72 runs along one side of the square.) In 4 miles, you'll come to the entrance to the **South Shore Unit** of **Choke Canyon State Park.** The development of this 385-acre park hasn't been completed, but there are facilities for fishing, boating, picknicking, and camping. The park consists of three units: the **Calliham Unit** and the **James E. Daugherty Wildlife Management Area** make up the other two. You'll pass the Calliham Unit, but the wildlife management area is not on this route, and offers no visitor facilities anyway. Its purpose is to provide a protected habitat for the study and preservation of the unique indigenous wildlife. Choke Canyon, for example, is as far west as American alligators have been seen.

From the South Shore Unit, you'll continue on Highway 72 past the Calliham Unit. You should stock up on water and snacks at the park store here, because there won't be another chance until you get to **Whitsett,** almost 25 miles away. In 4 more miles, you'll come to the third and last entrance into the state park, Park Road P7.

In 16 miles, you'll come to the intersection of Highway 72 and FM 99. Turn right on FM 99 and proceed north. You'll cross two bridges over the reservoir en route to the tiny town of Whitsett, 8 miles or so past the second bridge. There is a gas station/store there which is open 7 days a week. Whitsett was once the bee capital of South Texas, with a large apiary located there.

From Whitsett, turn right on Highway 281A, the old main Highway 281 which now serves as a bypass around the Highway 281/I-37. In 6 miles, Highway 281A will merge with Highway 281/I-37, and you should turn right and stay on the access road, which provides comfortable riding. In 3.5 miles, Highway 281 forks again, with I-37 going left and Highway 281 veering right and leading back to Three Rivers.

ACCOMMODATIONS: The Antler Inn, on Highway 281 (south of town across from the Diamond Shamrock Refinery), Three Rivers, (512) 786-2581.

CAMPING: Choke Canyon State Park, on Highway 72 (14.5 miles west of Three Rivers), Three Rivers, (512) 786-3868. **Tips State Park,** on Highway 72 and 1 mile off of Highway 281, Three Rivers, (512) 786-2528.

FOR MORE INFORMATION: Three Rivers Chamber of Commerce, P.O. Box 1648, Three Rivers, Texas, 78071, (512) 786-4330.

···

The South Padre Island Loop

The Rio Grande Valley is not really a valley at all—you'd need an observatory to see a mountain—but instead a fertile river delta. The Valley was created by the vast Rio Grande, which at this point nears the end of its 1,800-mile run through the Southwest to the Gulf of Mexico. The combination of mild, tropical climate and availability of irrigation water has turned the Valley into an agricultural mecca where more than 40 commercial crops, including everything from vegetables and citrus fruits to sugarcane and cotton, are grown. In addition, the valley's economy benefits from its proximity to the Gulf, and both Brownsville and Port Isabel house large shrimping fleets. The once booming off-shore oil industry is still evident, particularly around the Port of Brownsville, but it has declined with the rest of Texas' oil industry.

This ride begins and ends in **Los Fresnos,** a small farming community about 6 miles due north of Brownsville. Brownsville itself, a bustling city with the Mexican border town of Matamoros beckoning across the river, is busy, heavily trafficked, and a less desirable place to begin your ride than Los Fresnos. Avoid riding this area in July and August when the stifling tropical heat is at its worst, although even during these months the constant Gulf breezes will keep you from reaching total meltdown. Speaking of "breezes" (better known as headwinds), be prepared for them at all times of the year in this unbroken flatland.

Brownsville does have some points of interest, however, so if you want to explore the city before embarking, don't miss the **Gladys Porter Zoo,** at Ringgold Street and 6th Street. Call (210) 546-2177 for more information. It is a small but ingeniously laid out park consistently ranked as one of the ten best in the country. You might also want to visit **Fort Brown,** at 600 International (near the campus of **Texas Southmost College**), founded in 1846 just before the outbreak of the Mexican War. The fort hospital now serves as the school district's administration building. Also remaining are the post headquarters, guard house, medical laboratory, and morgue. The **Historic Brownsville Museum,** at East Madison Street and 6th Street, offers a permanent collection of documents, photos, furniture, and clothing from early Brownsville, as well as some yearly traveling exhibits. The Museum is housed in a 1928 railroad depot. Call (210) 548-1313 for hours.

To begin your ride, park in Los Fresnos and proceed west on Highway 100. This road will travel across *resacas* (canals and lagoons left over when the Rio Grande changed course), and through citrus groves and crop fields. These will gradually end as you near the marshes of the Gulf Coast. In 12.6 miles, you'll ride into **Laguna Vista.** Veer

- **Starting point:** Los Fresnos (loop)
- **Mileage:** 58 miles (or longer with option)
- **Terrain:** flat, but often with strong headwinds.
- **Best time to ride:** September through June
- **Traffic conditions:** heavy on Queen Isabella Causeway, but otherwise light to moderate.
- **Road conditions:** good

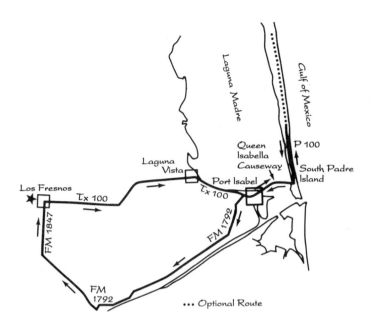

right, but stay on Highway 100 for 2.2 more miles into the bayside community of **Port Isabel.**

Port Isabel and its neighboring resort city of South Padre Island are the two largest communities on the very tip of Texas, but they are as different as salt and fresh water. Port Isabel is clearly a functional fishing community, with an impressive shrimp fleet at its port and numerous bait shops and fishing supply outlets along its main drag. South Padre Island is a playground, with condos and shell and surf shops clogging the 4 or 5 miles of island road.

For an overview of the **Queen Isabella Causeway,** the **Laguna Madre,** and **South Padre Island,** climb the 70 steps to the top of the old **Port Isabel Lighthouse,** which is on your right off of Highway 100 near the start of the causeway. Completed in 1853, it steered ships into the mouth of the Laguna Madre for half a century. Then plan a stop at the **Yacht Club,** at 700 Yturria Street. Call (210) 943-1301 to confirm hours. It is a fine old Spanish stucco-style hotel and restaurant that was built in the 1920s and is without a doubt one of the best places to eat native Gulf seafood on the Texas coast. Unfortunately, the restaurant is open for dinner only, but the hotel lobby, with its mounted trophy fish and pictures of early Port Isabel is worth a visit. And the food is worth driving back from wherever you're overnighting for dinner.

When you return to Highway 100 from the Yacht Club, turn toward the Queen Isabella Causeway. At this time, the causeway is designated closed to bikes, but because it is the only road to the island, this prohibition may be eliminated. Check with the Port Isabel Police Department (210-943-2283) to find out the latest status. If you do ride the 2.6 miles to South Padre Island, **use extreme caution!** Although a nicely paved, well-lighted four-lane causeway, it has a steady stream of fast-moving taffic. Always ride single file on the right shoulder, and if you can relax for a moment, enjoy the view. This causeway, which rises 73 feet above the high tide mark, is Texas' longest bridge.

Once you reach South Padre Island, turn left. This road, called Padre Boulevard, runs up the center of the narrow island. There is a nice shoulder, which you'll have to share with joggers, in-line skaters, and the like. Continue beyond the city limits, where civilization abruptly stops and you've got 10 miles of deserted road, sand dunes, and sea. To keep the mileage reasonable, this is a 10-mile round-trip jaunt. If you want to explore the road to its dead end, you'll add 10 miles to this ride.

When you're ready to turn around, follow the road back through South Padre Island, across the causeway, and into Port Isabel. Continue on Highway 100 (the main street) for 1.5 miles until it forks. Go left on FM 1792. You'll continue on FM 1792 for 10.3 miles past several inland salt bays and the Port of Brownsville. Just past the port, FM 1792 forks. Take the right fork and follow it until it hits FM 511; turn right. Follow FM 511 for 6 miles until it crosses FM 1847. Turn right and continue on FM 1847 for 4 miles into Los Fresnos.

ACCOMMODATIONS: Holiday Inn, 1945 North Expressway, Brownsville, (210) 546-4591. **Best Western,** 845 North Expressway, Brownsville, (210) 546-5501. For additional hotels and motels in Brownsville, call the **Brownsville Chamber of Commerce.**

FOR MORE INFORMATION: Brownsville Chamber of Commerce, 650 FM 802, P.O. Box 4697, Brownsville, Texas, 78523, (210) 546-3721 or 1-800-626-2639. **South Padre Island Tourist Bureau,** 600 Padre Boulevard, P.O. Box 3500, South Padre Island, Texas, 78597, (210) 761-6433 or 1-800-343-2368 (U.S. and Canada).

MAP
SOURCES

All of the following stores have an extensive selection of maps, which are also available through the mail.

Apache Trading Post
P.O. Box 997
Alpine, Texas 79831
(915) 837-5149
1-800-551-8217 (orders only)

Venture Map & Globe
2130 Highland Mall
Austin, Texas 78752
(512) 452-2326

One Map Place
212 Webb Chapel Village
Dallas, Texas 75220
(214) 241-2680

Allstate Map Company
1201 Henderson
Fort Worth, Texas 76102
(817) 332-1111

Key Maps Inc.
1411 West Alabama Street
Houston, Texas 77006
(713) 522-7949

Ferguson Maps
8131 I-10 West
San Antonio, Texas 78230
(210) 341-6277

CYCLING CLUBS AROUND THE STATE

Abilene Century Riders
1809 South Willis
Abilene, Texas 79605
Contact: Gary Stephenson
(915) 692-0293

Alamo City Athletic Club
3428 North St. Mary's
San Antonio, Texas 78212
Contact: Will Klein
(210) 732-1332

Alkek Velodrome
2999 South Wayside
Houston, Texas 77023
Contact: Kathy Volski
(713) 578-0858

Alpha Aces Velo, Inc.
4505 Willowbrook
Houston, Texas 77021
Contact: Alan-Alan Apurim
(713) 741-1458

A&M Cycling Team
Texas A&M University
College Station, Texas 77843
(409) 845-7826

Athens Bicycle Club
Box 2436
Athens, Texas 75751
Contact: Carl E. Tharp
(214) 677-3279

Baylor Cycling Team
Box 23261
Waco, Texas 76798
(817) 755-5761

Bayou Cycling Society
P.O. Box 2585
Baytown, Texas 77533
(713) 427-1195

Bell County Bicycle Club
Box 456
Nolanville, Texas 76559
(817) 699-3155

Big Country Bicycling
2300 Lincoln
Abilene, Texas 77601
Contact: Mike Kilmer
(915) 672-8777

Big Frank's Bicycling Club
2703 Montrose Boulevard
Houston, Texas 77006
Contact: John Hubert
(713) 523-6381

Bike Boerne
Box 1888
Boerne, Texas 78006
(210) 249-8000

Bluebonnet Council, A.Y.H.
5302 Crawford
Houston, Texas 77004
(713) 523-1009

Brazos Riders
2903 River Oaks Circle
Brazos, Texas 77802
(409) 846-2059

Brazosport Bicycle Club
110 Lake Jackson Road #407
Lake Jackson, Texas 77566
Contact: Richard Honea
(409) 299-1326

Caprock Cycling Club
P.O. Box 451
Crosbyton, Texas 79322
(806) 675-2940

Carrollton Cycling Club
3722 Penny Lane
Carrollton, Texas 75007
Contact: Bill Mugan
(214) 492-0856

Chaparral Cycling Club
5728 76th Street
Lubbock, Texas 79424
(806) 794-4492

Colorado River Cycling
919 Belvin
San Marcos, Texas 78666
Contact: Bill Glaze
(512) 357-2518

Corpus Christi Cycle Club
223 Oleander
Corpus Christi, Texas 78404
Contact: Alrae Huseman
(512) 888-9407

Dallas Area Tandem Enthusiasts
4252 Harvest Hill Road
Carrollton, Texas 75010
Contact: Bill or Debbie Bailey
(214) 492-2249

Dallas Off-Road Bicycle Association
18484 Preston Road #102-106
Dallas, Texas 75252
(214) 424-1066

Denton County Pedalers
Box 50442
Denton, Texas 76206
Contact: Darby Holland
(817) 387-9314

El Paso Bicycle Club
P.O. Box 13069
El Paso, Texas 79913
Contact: James Day
(915) 533-9698

Falcons Cycling Club
5008 Bissonnet
Bellaire, Texas 77401
Contact: Conrado Castano
(713) 665-3634

FBC Bike Club
7401 Katy Freeway
Houston, Texas 77024
Contact: Jose Votto
(713) 957-6700

Flatlanders Bicycling Association
913 South Fannin Street
Amarillo, Texas 79102
(806) 379-8747

Fort Worth Bicycling Association
P.O. Box 534
Fort Worth, Texas 76101
(817) 377-BIKR

Fort Worth Flyers Cycle Club
#16 Westcliff Center
Fort Worth, Texas 76109
(817) 377-BIKE

Fort Worth Road Club
3636 Meadowbrook Drive
Fort Worth, Texas 76103
Contact: Doug Punches
(817) 536-1444

Golden Triangle Cyclists
Box 3293
Port Arthur, Texas 77640
(713) 982-2255
(409) 866-4923

Greater Dallas Bicyclists
P.O. Box 12822
Dallas, Texas 75225
(214) 946-BIKE

Gulf Coast Cycling Association
2223 Bartlett
Houston, Texas 77098
(713) 691-3517

Houston Area Mountain Bike Rider Association
12260 Gulf Freeway
Houston, Texas 77034
Contact: George Rickard
(713) 943-7592

Houston Bicycle Club Inc.
Box 52752
Houston, Texas 77052
(713) 529-9709

Johnson Space Center Bicycle Club
Box 591101
Houston, Texas 77259
Contact: Bike Barn
(713) 480-9100

Lone Star Cyclists
Box 532141
Grand Prairie, Texas 75053
(214) 264-8648

Lone Star Sports Club
18219 Farnsfield Drive
Houston, Texas 77084
Contact: Stanton Truxillo
(713) 855-4859

Lubbock Bicycle Club
5409 86th Street
Lubbock, Texas 79424
(806) 798-RIDE

Matrix Cycling Club
Box 835801
Richardson, Texas 75083
Contact: Marc Mumby
(214) 358-4031

Mid-Cities Wheelman
1109 Woodvale Drive
Bedford, Texas 76021
Contact: Art Pacione
(817) 485-2407

Mirage Cycling Team
P.O. Box 181299
Dallas, Texas 75218
Contact: Richardson Bike Mart
(214) 327-6672

**Monahans Bicycle Association
(Broken Spokes)**
813 East Fourth Street
Monahans, Texas 79756
Contact: Dr. Gary Albertson
(915) 943-9477

North Austin Racing Team
906 West 24th
Austin, Texas 78705
Contact: Joel Rierson
(512) 343-7079

North Channel Bike Club
North Shore Schwinn
452 Uvalde
Houston, Texas 77015

North Texas Cyclists
Box 460802
Garland, Texas 75046
Contact: Tom Boydon
(214) 278-0111

Northwest Cycling Club
17458 Northwest Freeway
Houston, Texas 77040
Contact: Randy Meeks
(713) 466-1240

Pasadena Pedalers
Pasadena Library
20495 Richey
Pasadena, Texas 77504
(713) 472-6651

Pedalers Bicycle Club
P.O. Box 2909, MS 2225
Austin, Texas 78769
Contact: Bill Prout
(512) 250-7676

Peloton Racing Organization
616 West 34th Street
Austin, Texas 78705
Contact: Don Hutchinson
(512) 441-0661

**Permian Basin Bicycle
Association**
Box 5679
Midland, Texas 79711
Contact: John Bearne
(915) 699-1719

**Pineywoods Pedalers Bicycle
Club**
508C East Denman
Lufkin, Texas 75901
Contact: C.B. Burris
(409) 632-4308

Plano Athletic Cycling Club
605 East 18th
Plano, Texas 75074
Contact: Rick Gurney
(214) 424-4130

Possum Pedalers Bicycle Club
P.O. Box 1101
Graham, Texas 76046
Contact: Randy Stephens
(817) 549-3918

Post Pedalers
P.O. Box 296
Post, Texas 79356
(806) 495-2000

Red River Cycle Club
125 Northeast 27th
Paris, Texas 75260
Contact: Eddie McFadden
(214) 784-4119

Rice University Cycling Team
Box 1892
Houston, Texas 755251
Contact: Garrick Mitchell
(713) 630-8147

S.A.B.A.R. Triathlon Club
2833 Stoneridge
Garland, Texas 75044
Contact: Kerry Kinny or Mary Orr
(214) 826-4059

**San Angelo Bicycling
Association**
Box 60942
San Angelo, Texas 76906
Contact: Terry Doyal
(915) 944-2947

San Antonio Bicycle Racing Club
428 Cloverleaf #1
San Antonio, Texas 78209
Contact: Roland Wilson
(210) 671-3881

San Antonio Wheelmen
Box 34208
San Antonio, Texas 78265
(210) 828-2717

Sandhill Cyclists
213 East Fifth
Olton, Texas 79064
(806) 285-2731

South Texas Area Racing Team
Velo Sports Bicycle Shop
3825 South Staples
Corpus Christi, Texas 78411
Contact: John Bratton
(512) 852-4301

Southwest Schwinn Riding Club
6607 Braeswood
Houston, Texas 77096
(713) 777-5333

**Sun & Ski Sports
Cycling Club**
6100 Westheimer #126
Houston, Texas 77057
(713) 378-8180

SWT Cycling Team
3008 L.B.J.S.C.
San Marcos, Texas 78666
Contact: Preston Patton
(512) 629-5508

Team El Paso Bicycling Club
6800 Gateway East
El Paso, Texas 79925
Contact: Hy Silverstein
(915) 595-6900

Team Jonti
(Jack Johnston Bicycles)
7820 Garland Road
Dallas, Texas 75218
Contact: Jack Johnston
(214) 328-5238

Team McAllen
1515 Hawk Circle
McAllen, Texas 78504
(512) 687-9045

**Team Rockwall/Bicycle
Emporium Club**
2006 South Goliad
Rockwall, Texas 75087
Contact: Carolyn Armstrong
(214) 722-0207

Team Shock
Bicycle Exchange
1305 South Broadway
Carrollton, Texas 75006
Contact: Rusty Roberts
(213) 242-4209

Texarkana Bicycle Club
2620 Summer Hill Road
Texarkana, Texas 75501
Contact: Jack Fisher
(214) 793-3271

Texas Eagles Cycling Club
4434 Steffani Lane
Houston, Texas 77041
Contact: Herman Vasquez
(713) 442-4528

Texas Flyers
1204 North Stemmons
Lewisville, Texas 75057
Contact: Ben Hayes
(214) 221-9322

Texas Road Club
8140 Walnut Hill #1001, LB 60
Dallas, Texas 75231
Contact: David McBee
(214) 739-0707 or
James Burnett
(817) 936-6028

Texas Tech Cycling Team
Texas Tech University 4390
Lubbock, Texas 79406
(806) 742-3351

Texas Velodrome Association
12 Leverwood Court
The Woodlands, Texas 77381
(713) 292-5995

Texas Velos
8640 Beauregard
Dallas, Texas 75225
Contact: Brent Fereck
(214) 361-5254

Texas Wheels Cycling Club
P.O. Box 5586
Arlington, Texas 76005
Contact: Lisa Richards/Wheels
in Motion
(817) 860-2991

Tomball Country Cyclists
Texas Sports Medicine Center
28120 Tomball Parkway
Tomball, Texas 77375
Contact: Tom Dolan
(713) 351-6300

Trinity Cycling Club
Trinity University
715 Stadium Drive Box 398
San Antonio, Texas 78212
(512) 737-4048

Tyler Bicycle Club
P.O. Box 6734
Tyler, Texas 75711
Contact: John Schofield
(903) 581-0225

U.T. Cycling Club
Gregory #33
Austin, Texas 78712
(512) 495-5174

Uvalde Bicycle Racing Club
113 North Getty
Uvalde, Texas 78801
(512) 278-4634

Violet Crown Sports Association
Box 3479
Austin, Texas 78764
Contact: William Chambers
(512) 441-8648

Waco Bicycle Club
Box 2570
Waco, Texas 76702
Contact: Cindy Neal
(817) 772-7150

West-End Mountain Bike Club
5427 Blossom
Houston, Texas 77007
Contact: Chad Kennedy
(713) 861-2271

Wichita Falls Bicycling Club
P.O. Box 2096
Wichita Falls, Texas 76307
Contact: Chuck Foley
(817) 696-1505

Williamson County Cycling Association
Box 1176
Round Rock, Texas 78680
Contact: Tom Purdy
(512) 244-1232

Wimberley Cycling Association
Box 12
Wimberley, Texas 78676
Contact: Tom Jacob
(512) 847-2201

NOTES

NOTES

NOTES

NOTES

About the Authors

Ann K. Baird has been involved in serious cycling for eight years. She rides about 5,000 miles a year competitively and recreationally and has completed many centuries. She has also pedaled all over the United States and Europe and has led tours in New York, California, and Idaho. As a past chair of the Texas Bicycle Coalition (an advocacy organization) and vice president of the Houston Bicycle Club, she now chairs the Bicycle Rules Advisory Committee to the Texas Department of Transportation. She lives in Houston, Texas, with her husband and eight-year-old son.

Rebecca Kinserlow has been cycling seriously for five years and is a past president of the Lubbock Bicycle Club. As a West Texas native, she regularly traverses the quiet canyons of the Panhandle. Once a year in February, she completes a grueling ten-day tour through Big Bend National Park. She lives in Lubbock, Texas.

George Sevra began bicycling in 1980 to augment his mountaineering training. Shortly thereafter, he was invited on a tour to Orcas Island in the San Juan Islands of Washington with the Canadian Youth Hosteling Association. The rest, as they say, is history because he has not been climbing since. He is also the author of *A Guide to Bicycling in Texas*, which he researched by riding nearly 4,000 miles.

Ed Swan is a 39-year-old veteran cyclist, coming up on his tenth year in the sport, who considers himself a racing tourist or a touring racer depending on who he's chasing. He has toured in nine states, Canada, and one former republic . . . Texas! He is a charter member of the board of directors of the Texas Bicycle Coalition and an officer of the Fort Worth Bicycling Association. He has written for regional and national cycling publications. He also writes a weekly cycling column for the *Fort Worth Star Telegram*. He lives in Fort Worth, Texas, with his wife, Suzie, who is an intermediate-school principal and the most understanding and tolerant non-cycling spouse in the world.

Lawrence Walker took his first bicycle tour (from Dallas to Austin) in 1974, at the age of 16. In the early 1980s, he designed the 1,100-mile Trans Texas Trail from El Paso to Orange, and led the first Trans Texas Tour for the state's sesquicentennial in April 1986. As founder and director of Coyote Bicycle Tours (formerly Lone Star Bicycle Tours—for more information, write P.O. Box 1832, Austin, Texas, 78767), he has led more than 30 tours in Texas, New Mexico, California, and the West and continues to lead several popular tours each year. His cycling friends and tour participants call him "Mr. Triple T" (a nickname from the Trans Texas Tour days) or, simply, "Leader Guy." Lawrence is also a freelance writer and cultural historian, specializing in Southwestern art, geography, national parks and monuments, pop culture, and travel. He lives in Austin, Texas.

☐

Peter Nye's articles on cycling have been published in *Sports Illustrated, Women's Sports & Fitness, USA Today, The Washington Post,* and several dozen other publications. His books include *Hearts of Lions: The Story of American Bicycle Racing, The Cyclist's Sourcebook,* and *Never Give Up: The Saga of John Howard, the Fastest Bicycle Rider in the World.*